JeAn BoNnIn

A wELSh SuRRealist

"THROUGH A COMBINATION OF
HARD WORK AND SERENDIPITY
I HAVE ACHIEVED ANONYMITY
IN
NEW YORK
PARIS
BERLIN
LONDON
AND   WALES."

JEAN BONNIN
MARCH 2018
(AS QUOTED FROM
THE MALCOLM
DE CHAZAL
EXHIBITION
CATALOGUE
2018)

A Welsh Surrealist

An Original Publication of Black Egg Publishing

An imprint of Black Egg Publishing

First published in the UK by Black Egg Publishing

in 2018

www.redeggpublishing.com

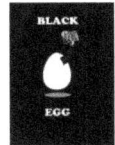

Copyright © Jean Bonnin 2018

Jean Bonnin has asserted his moral right to be identified as the author of this book

Cover design: Black Egg Publishing

British Library Cataloguing-in-Publication Data

A catalogue record for this book is available upon

request from the British Library

ISBN: 978-1-9998215-0-0

While every effort has been made to contact any possible copyright-holders, if an acknowledgement has been overlooked, please contact the publisher. Any copyright infringements will be purely unintentional. Please contact the publisher and any issues will be resolved immediately.

This book is sold subject to the condition that it shall not, by way of trade or otherwise, be lent, re-sold, hired out, or otherwise circulated without the publisher's prior consent in any form of binding or cover other than that in which it is published and without a similar condition including this condition being imposed on the subsequent purchaser

JEAN BONNIN

(ARTIST, NOVELIST, POET AND MUSICIAN)

JEAN BONNIN WAS BORN IN PARIS, FRANCE, IN MAY 1968. AS THE UPRISING WAS TAKING PLACE THROUGHOUT THE CAPITAL AND, TO GREATER OR LESSER EXTENTS, THROUGHOUT THE GLOBE, SO THE YOUNG BONNIN WAS RISING UP INTO A NEW WORLD. A WORLD OF HOPE AND OPTIMISM, FILLED WITH ALL THE POSSIBILITIES THAT THE FUTURE COULD HOLD FOR TEARING UP THE RULEBOOK AND STARTING AGAIN. . . JEAN, THEN, BEGAN HIS LIFE HOW HE LIVED IT:

READY FOR REVOLUTION AND CHANGE. . .   OF ALL KINDS!

BIOGRAPHY

AFTER, AND WHILE, STUDYING POLITICS AND POLITICAL PHILOSOPHY AT VARIOUS UNIVERSITIES BONNIN JOINED A NUMBER OF PUNK BANDS. AFTER THIS HE MOVED TO NORTHERN FRANCE, AND SUBSEQUENTLY TO BERLIN AND THE FORMER EAST GERMANY. HE BECAME INVOLVED WITH THE AVANT-GARDE AND UNDERGROUND MUSIC SCENES. AT THE SAME TIME AS THIS HE BEGAN WRITING HIS FIRST NOVEL. AND IT WAS ALSO DURING THIS PERIOD THAT HE BEGAN TO TAKE HIS ARTWORK MORE SERIOUSLY (IN AN ANTI-SERIOUS MANNER) - AT FIRST DESIGNING THE ALBUM COVERS, FLIERS AND POSTERS FOR THE VARIOUS MUSIC GROUPS HE WAS EITHER INVOLVED WITH OR KNEW.

STILL LIVING IN THE FORMER EAST GERMANY, SURROUNDED BY EASTERN BLOC MINIMALISM AND CONSTRUCTIVISM, HE BEGAN EXHIBITING HIS WORKS IN SMALL BACKSTREET GALLERIES. SOMETIMES HE WOULD PROVIDE THE BACKGROUND MUSIC FOR THE EXHIBITION, AND USUALLY HE WOULD DESIGN AND DISTRIBUTE THE FLIERS THAT ANNOUNCED TO PEOPLE THAT SOMETHING POSSIBLY SIGNIFICANT WAS OCCURRING IN AN OTHERWISE INSIGNIFICANT STREET... HE WASN'T VERY SUCCESSFUL HOWEVER AND HENCE AFTER A COUPLE OF YEARS DECIDED TO CONCENTRATE ON HIS WRITING...

YEARS LATER, HAVING HAD SEVERAL OF HIS NOVELS, POETRY BOOKS AND TRANSLATIONS PUBLISHED, HE DECIDED TO RETURN TO HIS ARTWORK.

WITHIN THE SPACE OF THREE YEARS BONNIN HAD HAD HIS WORKS EXHIBITED IN TWELVE EXHIBITIONS BOTH IN WALES AND INTERNATIONALLY...

INFLUENCES

SOMEWHAT ASTONISHINGLY JEAN BONNIN'S FIRST MEMORY WAS OF THE MOON LANDING. HE RECOUNTS HOW HE WAS PLACED ON HIS WELSH GRANDFATHER'S KNEE TO WATCH THE BROADCAST. HIS GRANDFATHER TURNED TO HIM AND TOLD HIM TO "REMEMBER THIS... IT'S IMPORTANT". AND SO HE DID...

APART FROM THE SPACE-AGE HE HAS CITED THE FOLLOWING AS HAVING BEEN SIGNIFICANT INFLUENCES ON HIS THOUGHT PROCESSES, AND SUBSEQUENTLY, ONE CAN PRESUME, ON BOTH HIS WRITING AND HIS ARTWORK:
THE FIRST TIME HE HEARD THE CLASH'S EPONYMOUS FIRST ALBUM; ALSO LISTENING TO CAN, AND FAUST, AND P.I.L., AND THROBBING GRISTLE, AND EINSTÜRZENDE NEUBAUTEN, AND THE FALL... AND DAVID BOWIE. COMING ACROSS TERRY RILEY'S *IN C* FOR THE FIRST TIME WAS ALSO AN INFLUENTIAL MOMENT... AS WAS LISTENING TO KARLHEINZ STOCKHAUSEN ON AN OLD WALKMAN WHILST WAITING FOR A STRASSENBAHN ON A RAIN-FILLED FEBRUARY NIGHT IN BERLIN.

READING BURROUGHS, AUSTER, GOGOL, HUXLEY, DE NERVAL, ARTAUD, DE CHAZAL, WITTGENSTEIN, NIETZSCHE, BRUNO SCHULZ, MIKHAIL BULGAKOV, ORWELL, THE CUT-UP METHOD (EMPLOYED BY MANY MANY)...........
....

AND, OF COURSE, THERE WERE MANY ARTISTS AND ARTISTIC MOVEMENTS THAT INFLUENCED BONNIN'S WORK. THOUGH POLITICS AND MUSIC WERE AS STRONG, IF NOT STRONGER, INFLUENCES ON BONNIN'S WORK... WE COULD NONETHELESS MENTION FUTURISM, THE COBRA ART MOVEMENT, PUNK ARTWORK, DADA, POP-ART, PREHISTORIC ART, ABSTRACT IMPRESSIONISM, AND OF COURSE SURREALISM...
BUT ALL OF THIS SEEMS TO MATTER LITTLE. WHAT MATTERS MORE IS THAT BONNIN IS ECLECTIC, DIVERSE, ANARCHIC, COMPLETELY ORIGINAL AND FULL OF FUN.

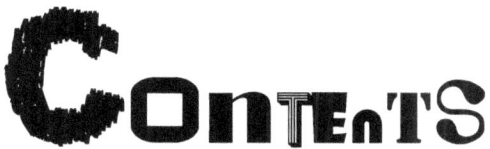

Contents

INSIDE YOU WILL FIND A COLLECTION OF BONNIN'S VISUAL WORK (EXCLUDING IMAGES OF HIS SCULPTURES AND READYMADES)... REGRETTABLY THE PUBLISHERS HAVE BEEN UNABLE TO TRACK DOWN A LARGE AMOUNT OF BONNIN'S EARLIER WORK FOR THIS EDITION. WE HOPE TO RECTIFY THIS EITHER FOR FUTURE EDITIONS OR FOR A SEPARATE VOLUME.

WHAT YOU WILL FIND BETWEEN THE COVERS OF THIS BOOK IS :- ANTI-RELIGION, ANTI-BOURGEOIS, ANTI-CAPITALIST, ANTI-INEQUALITY, ANTI-FASCIST, ANTI-MONOTONY; PRO IMAGINATION, PRO RANDOMNESS, PRO FREEDOM, PRO SUBVERSION, PRO RADICALISM, PRO LOVE...

PUT ON YOUR 4D GLASSES NOW

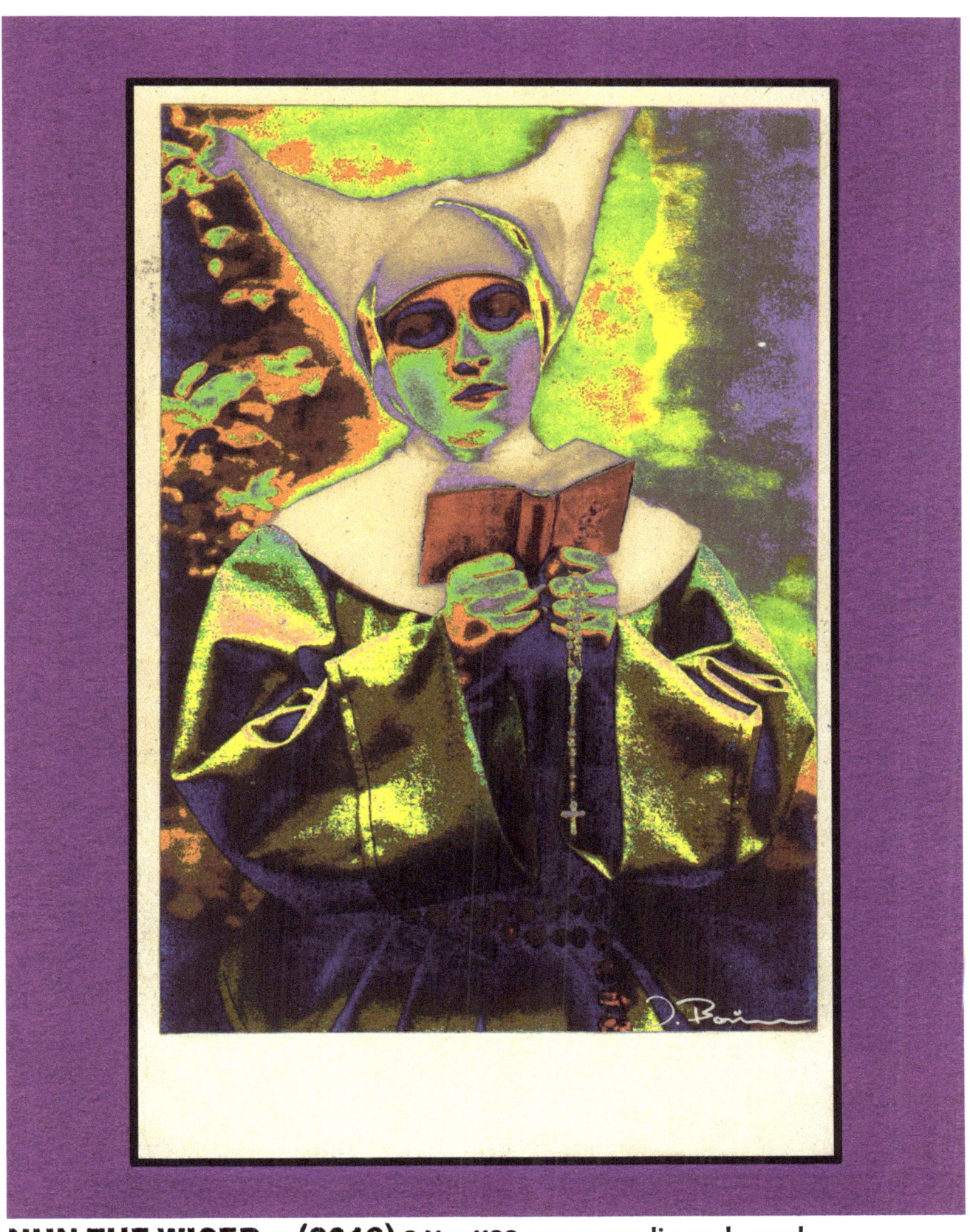

NUN THE WISER – (2016) 841 x 1189 mm, acrylic on board, photographed with treatments

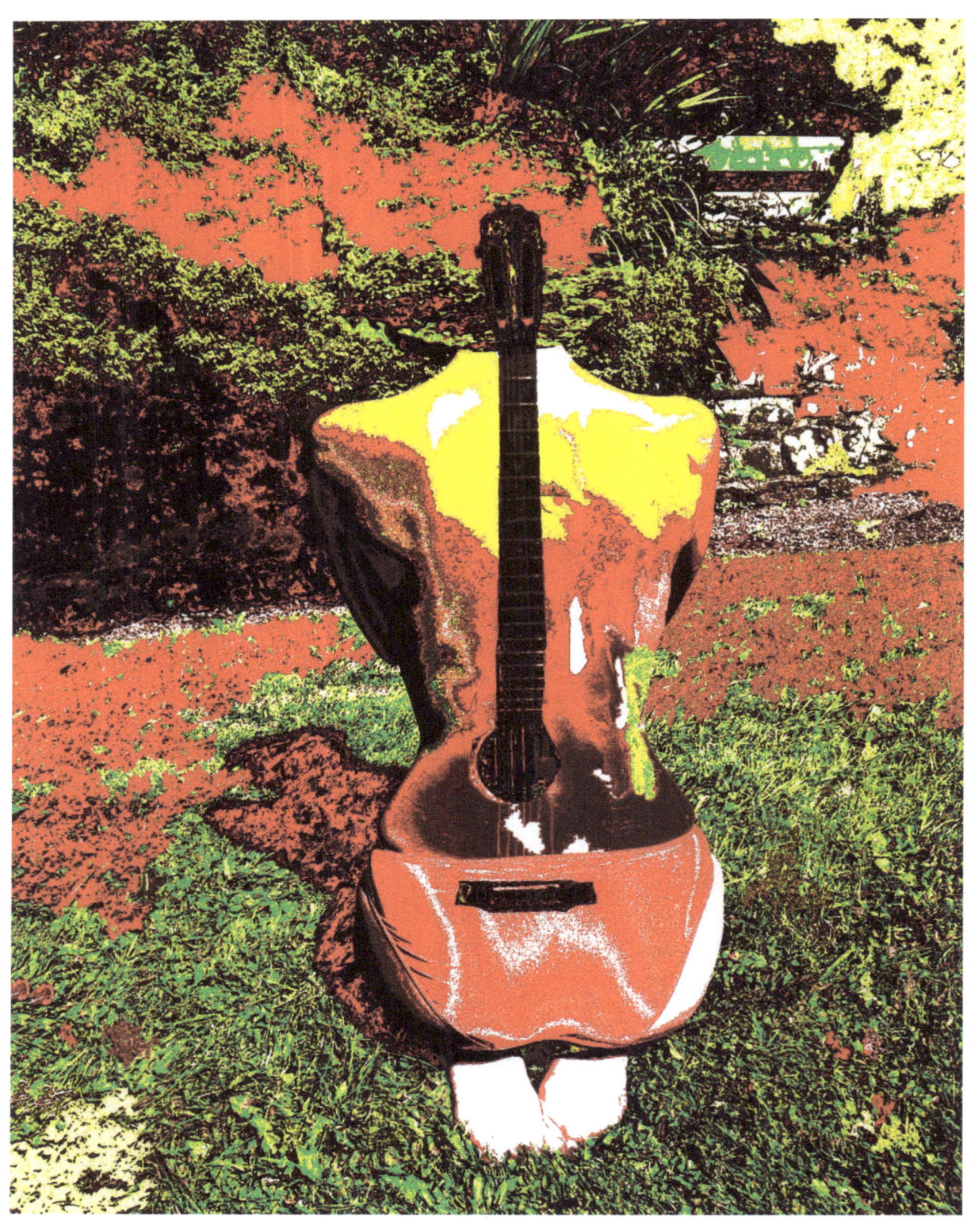

GUITAR (RED) - (2015) 841 x 1189 mm, photograph with treatments

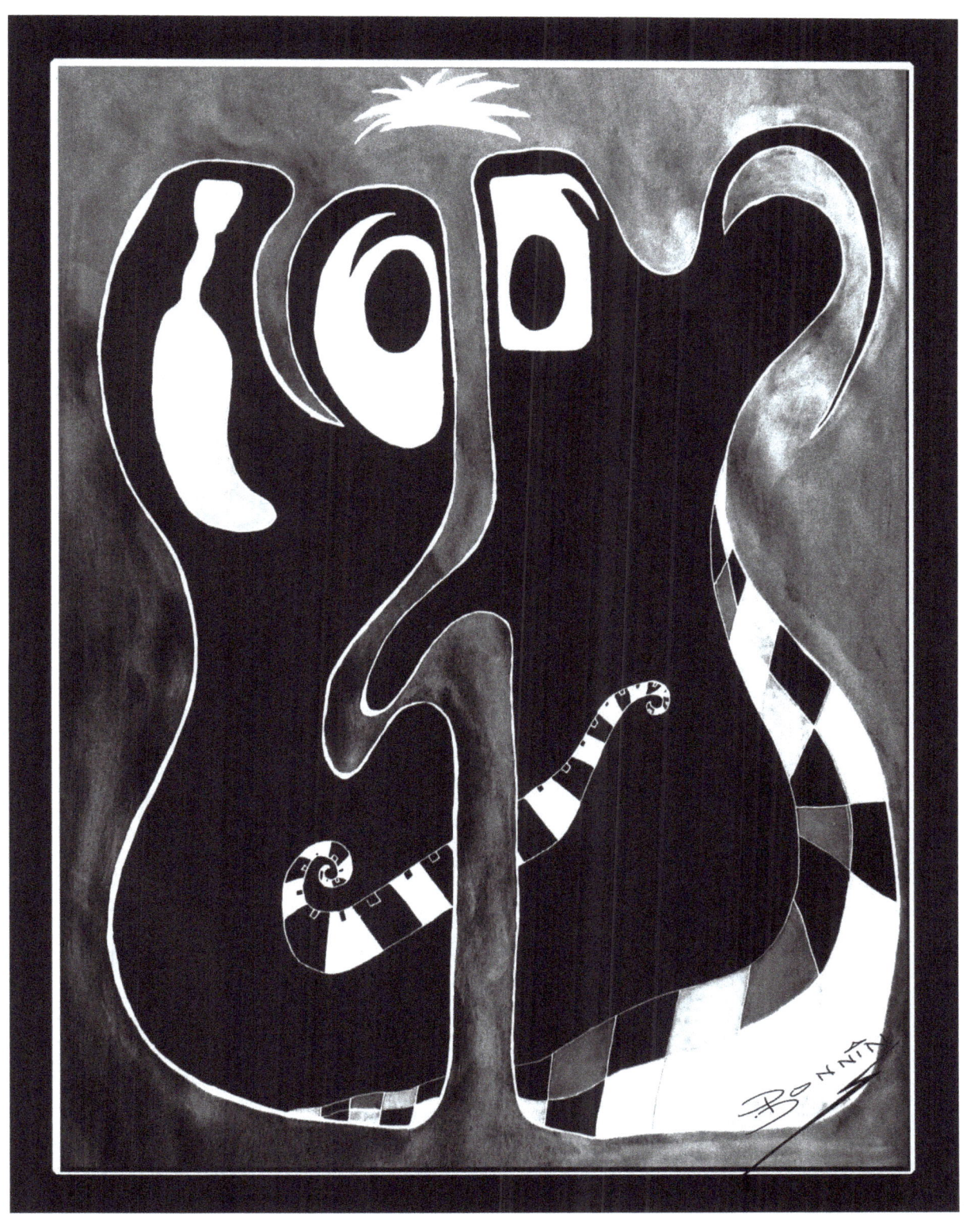

PIANO-MOUTH 2 - (1998) 297 x 420 mm, pencils and acrylic on paper, photographed

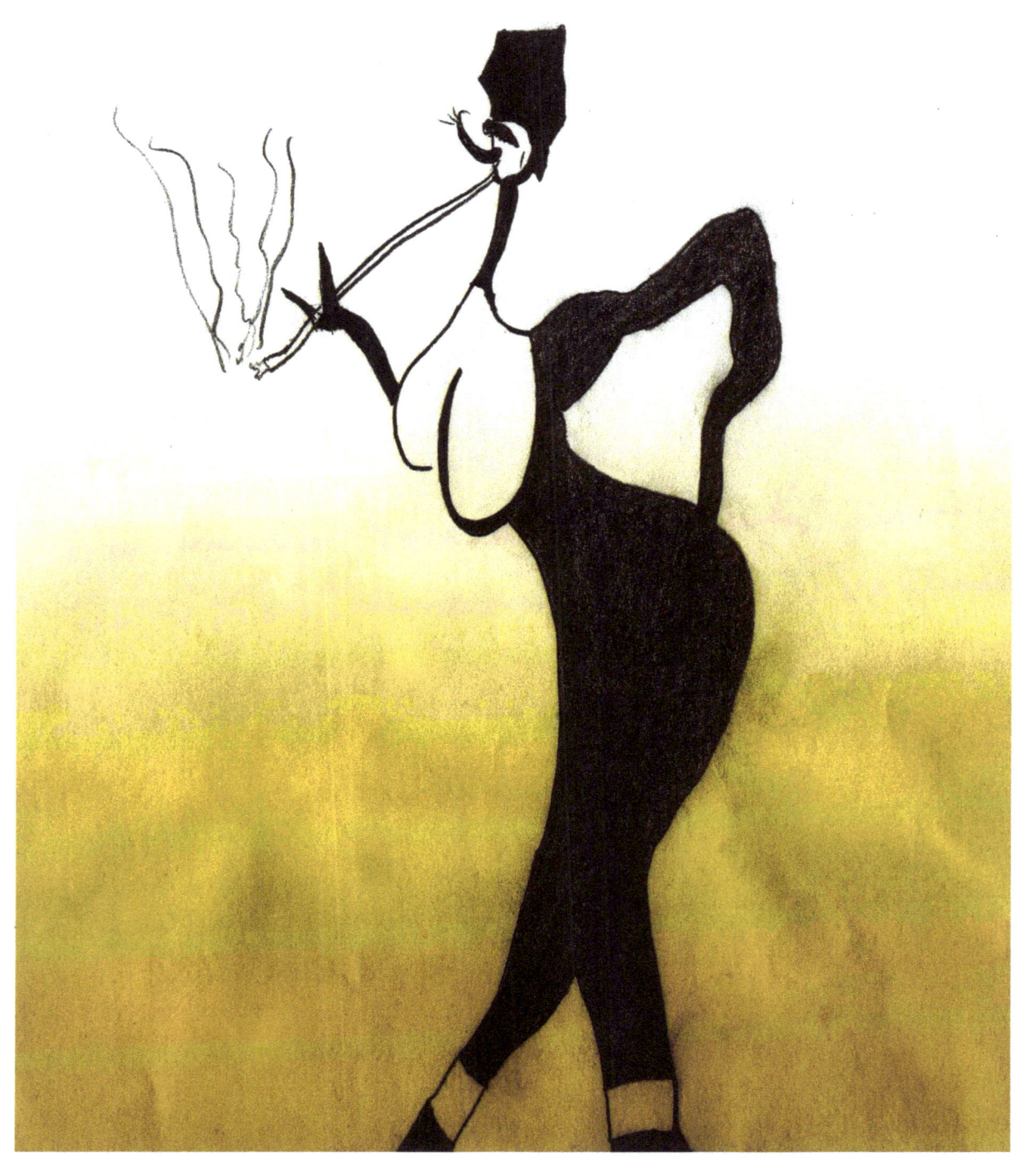

TALL WOMAN 2 - (1984) 297 x 420 mm, pencils on paper

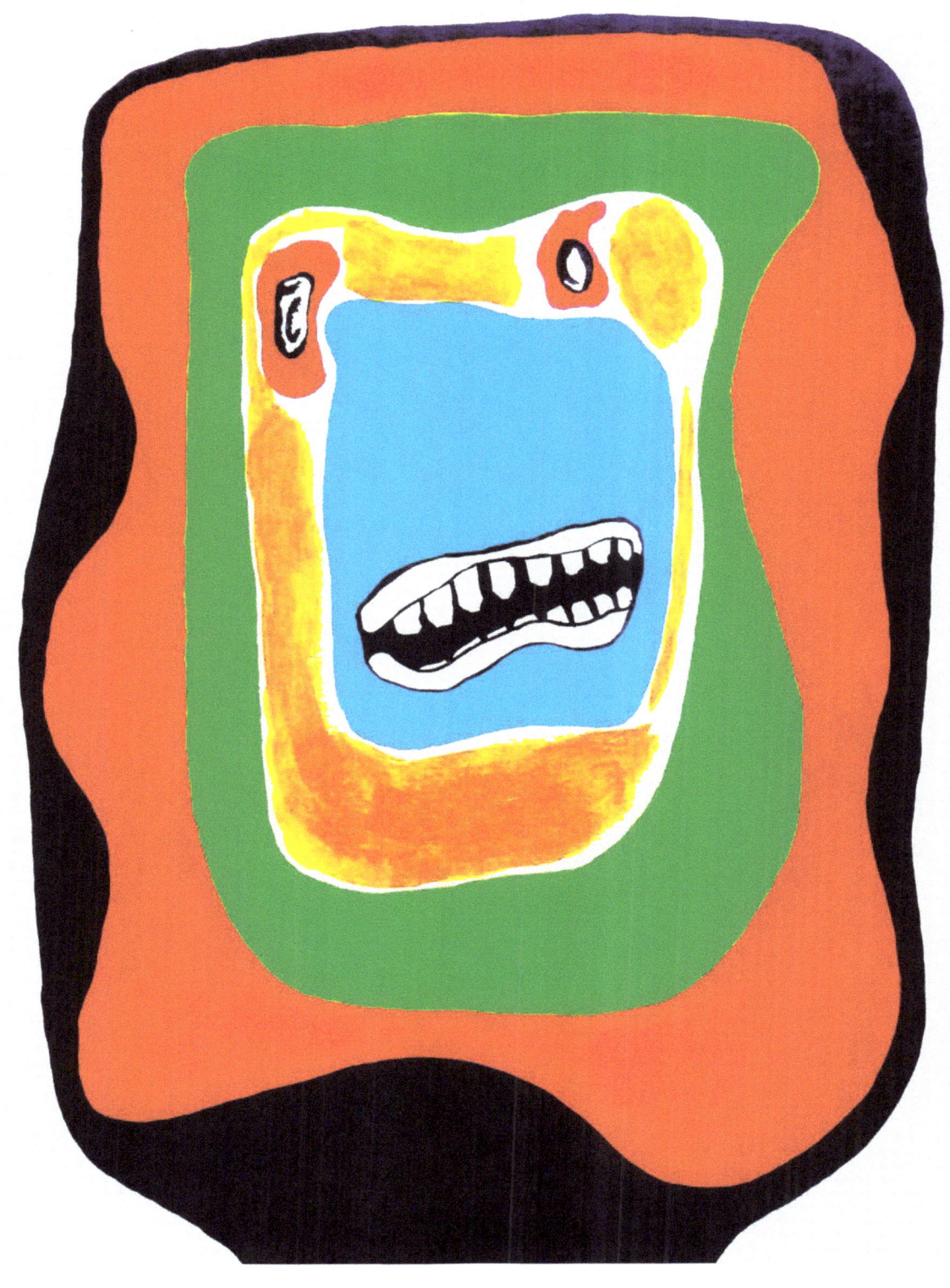

SQUARE-HEAD - (2001) 297 x 420 mm, acrylic on board, photographed

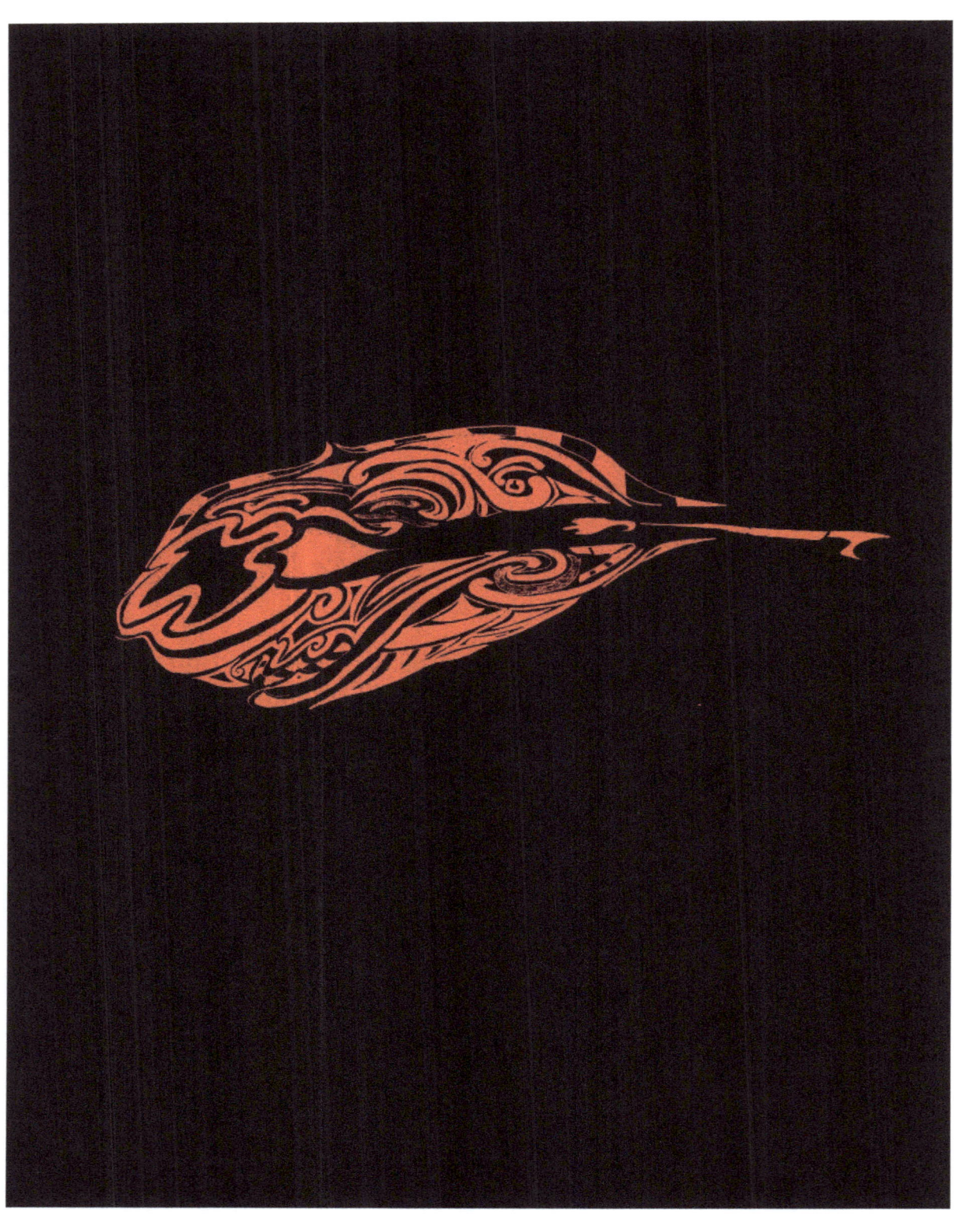

UNTITLED - (1982) 297 x 420 mm, acrylic and pencil on board, photographed with slight treatments

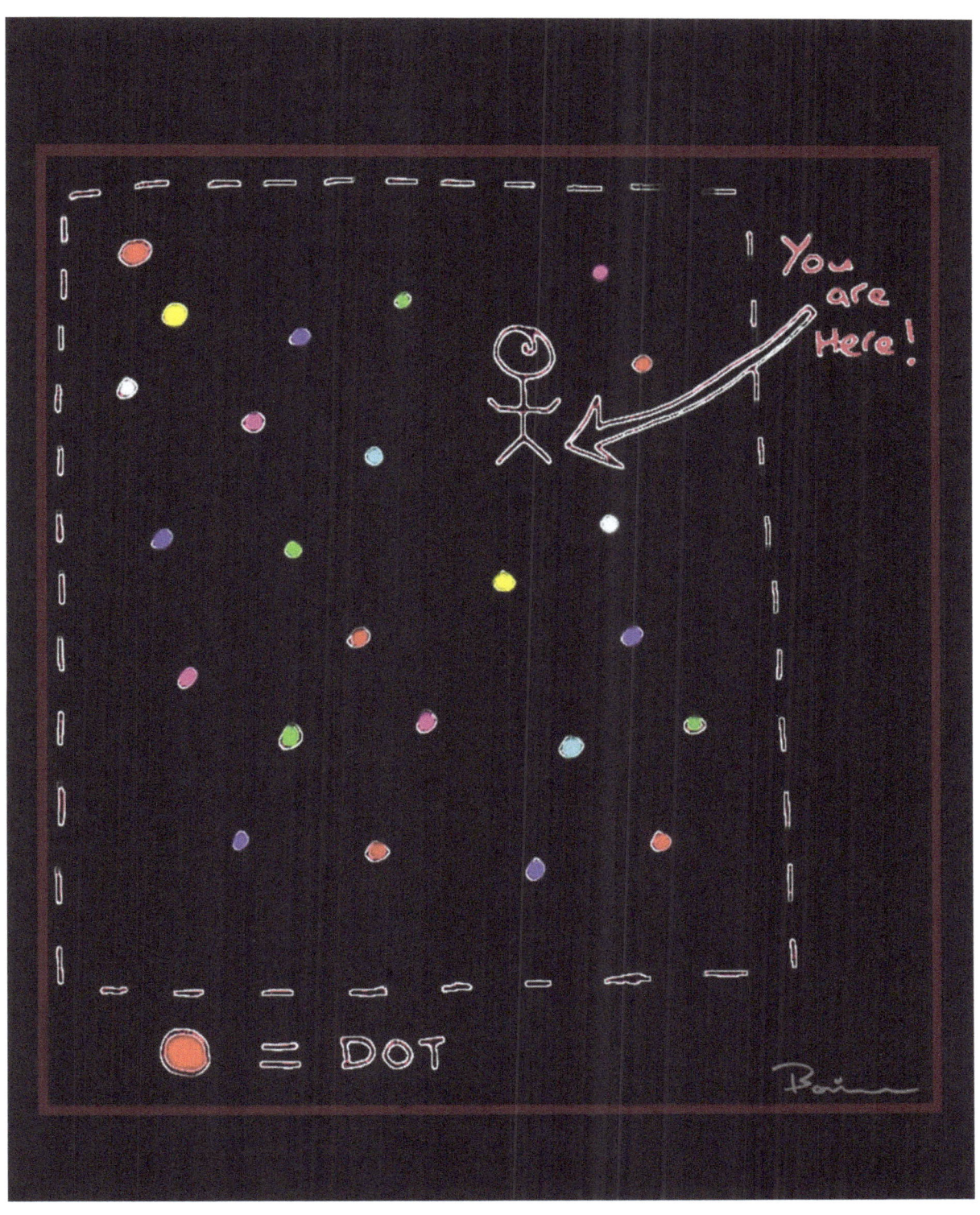

DOT EQUALS DOT - (2008) 297 x 420 mm, pencils on paper, with slight after-treatments

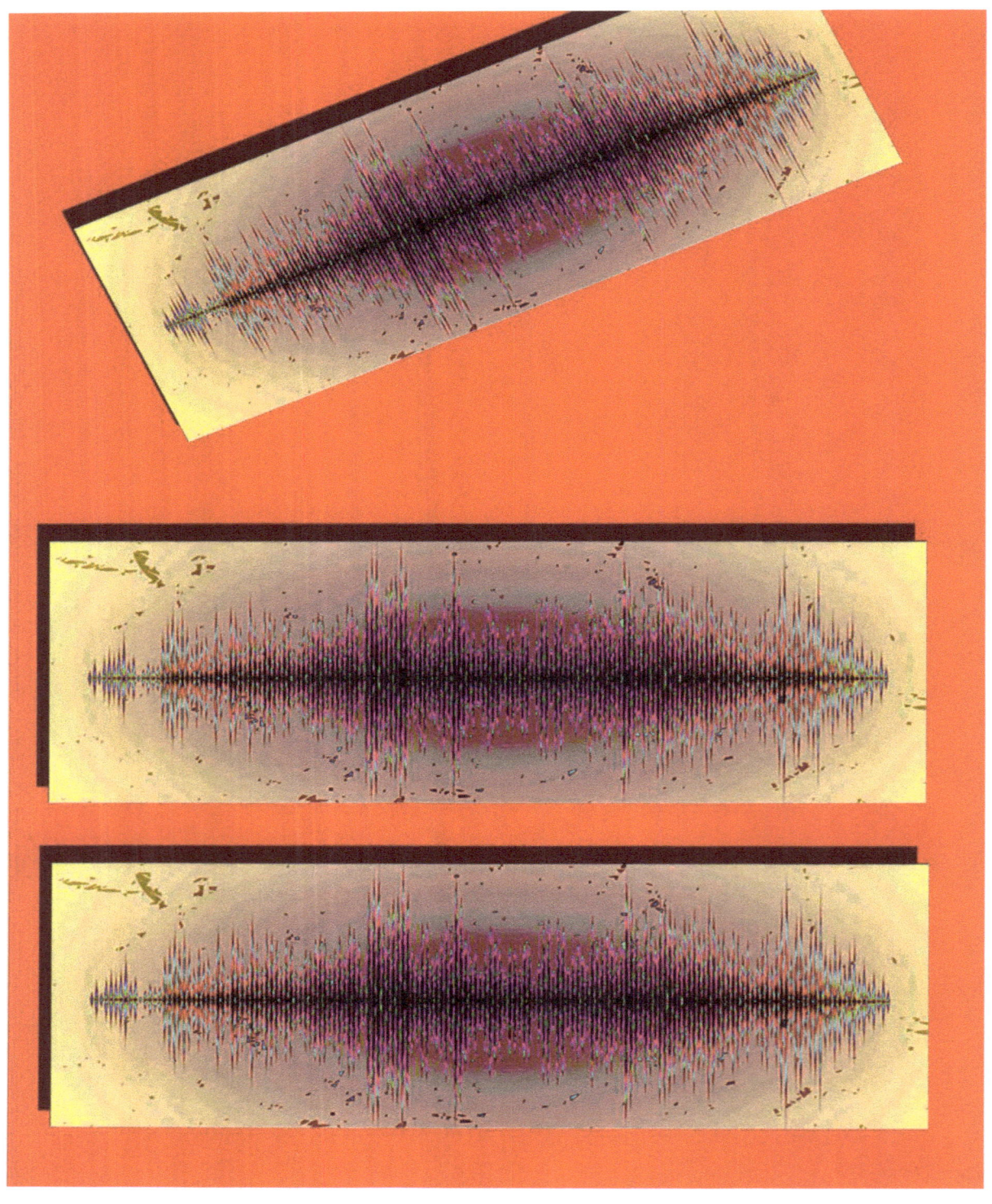

THE SOUND OF A KISS (2018) soundwave, photographed and treated

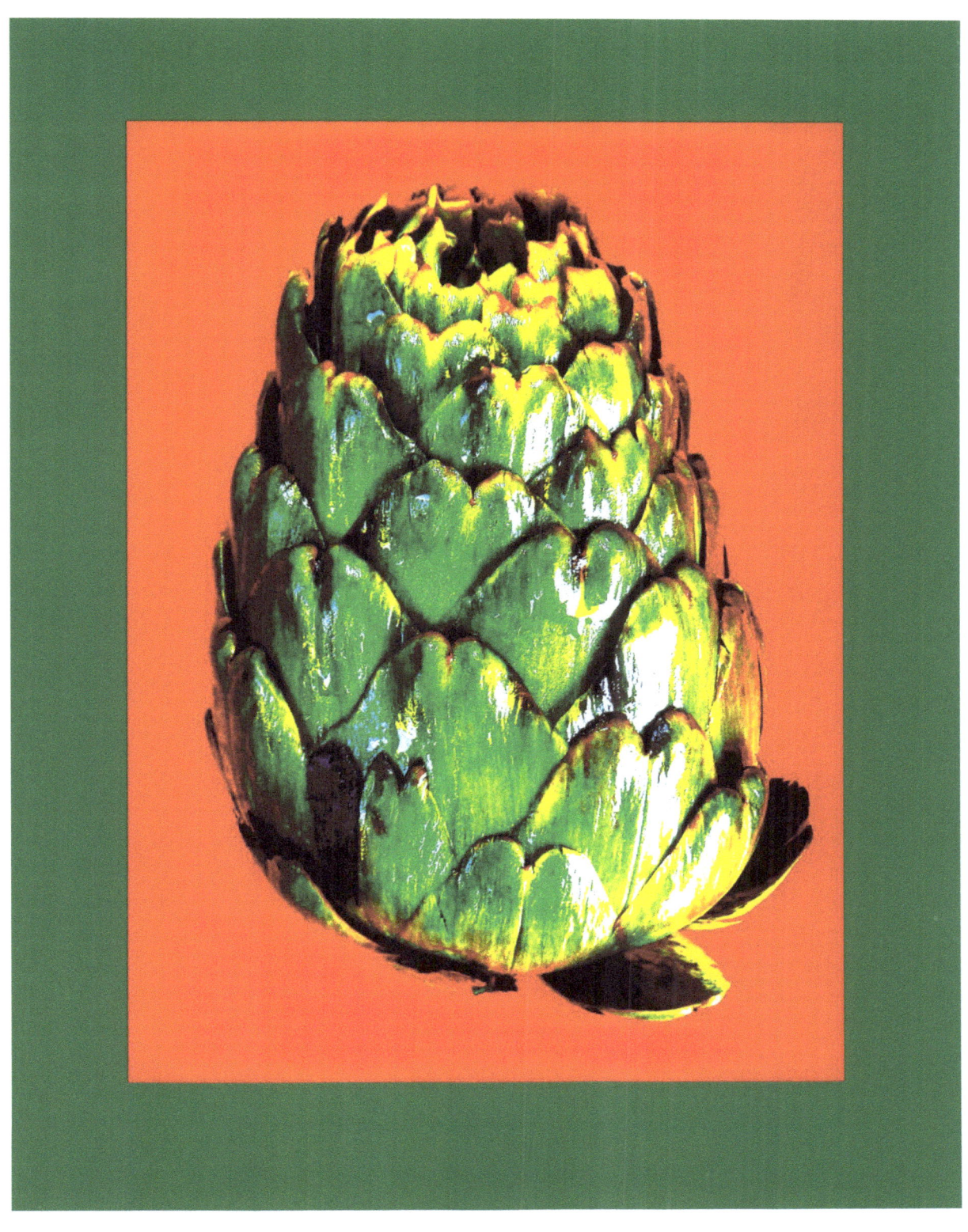

ARTICHOKE - (CIRCA **2013**) forgotten techniques

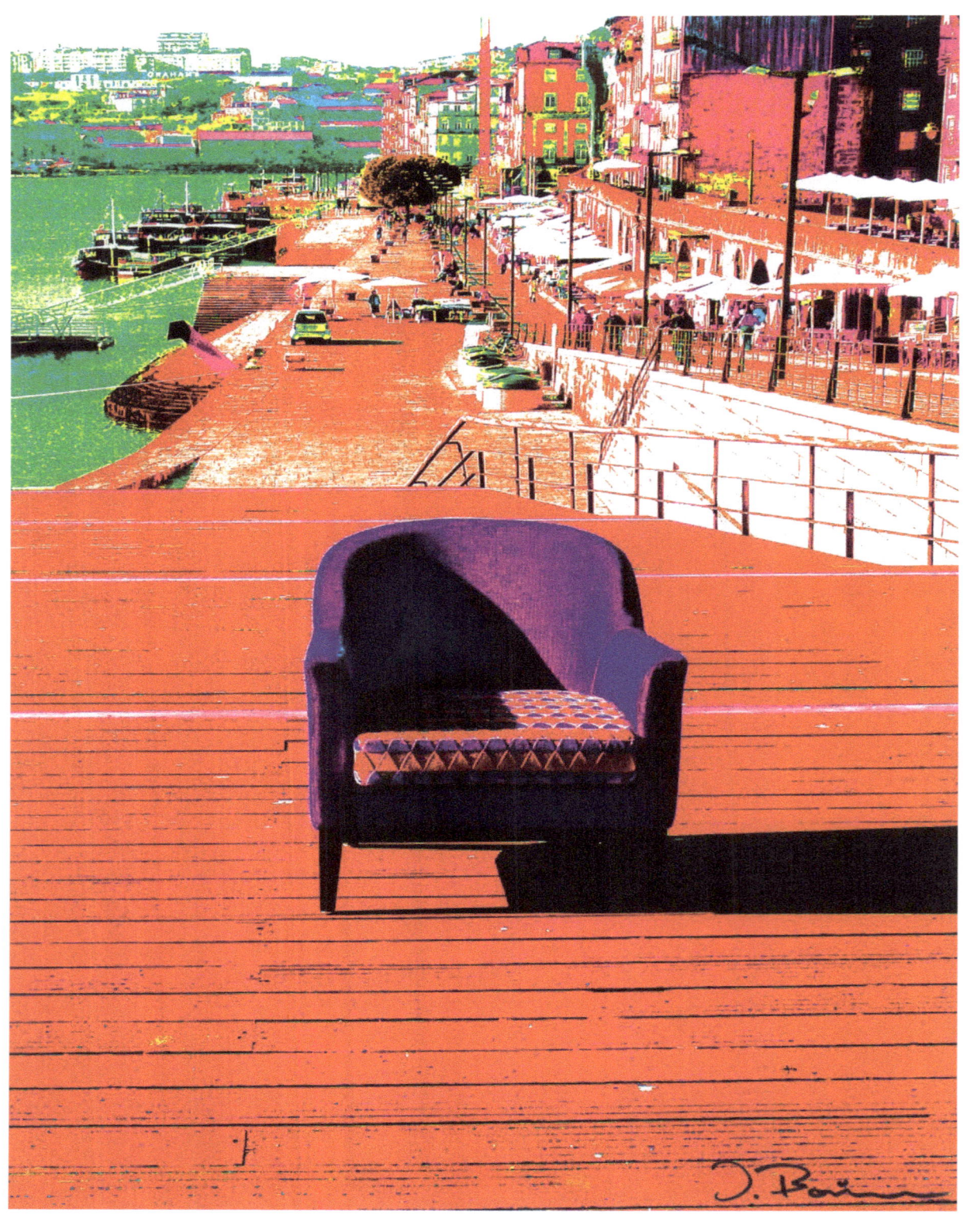

CHAIR (RED) - (2014) photograph, paint and treatments

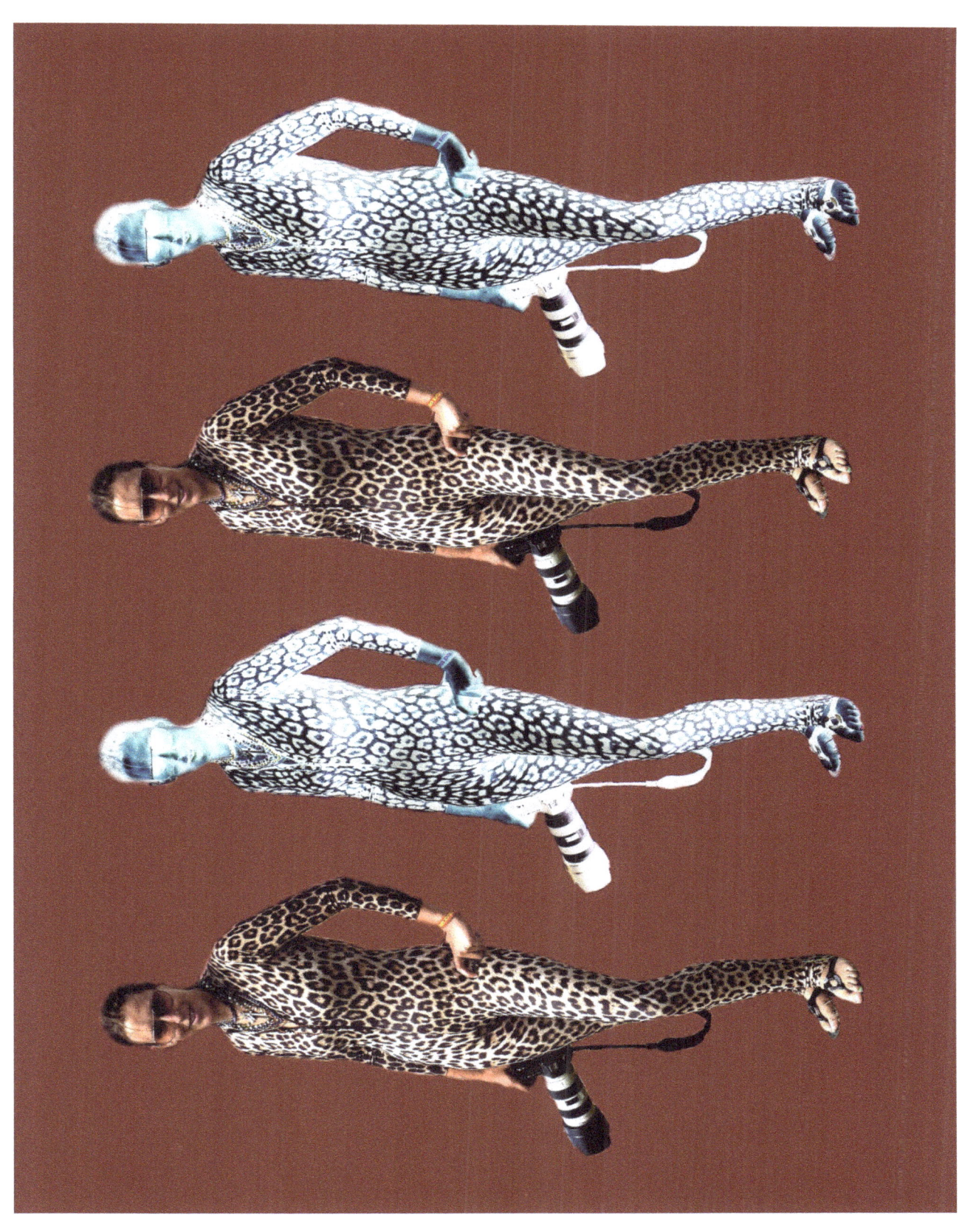

LEOPARD WOMAN 2 - (2010 & 2018) photograph and Treatments

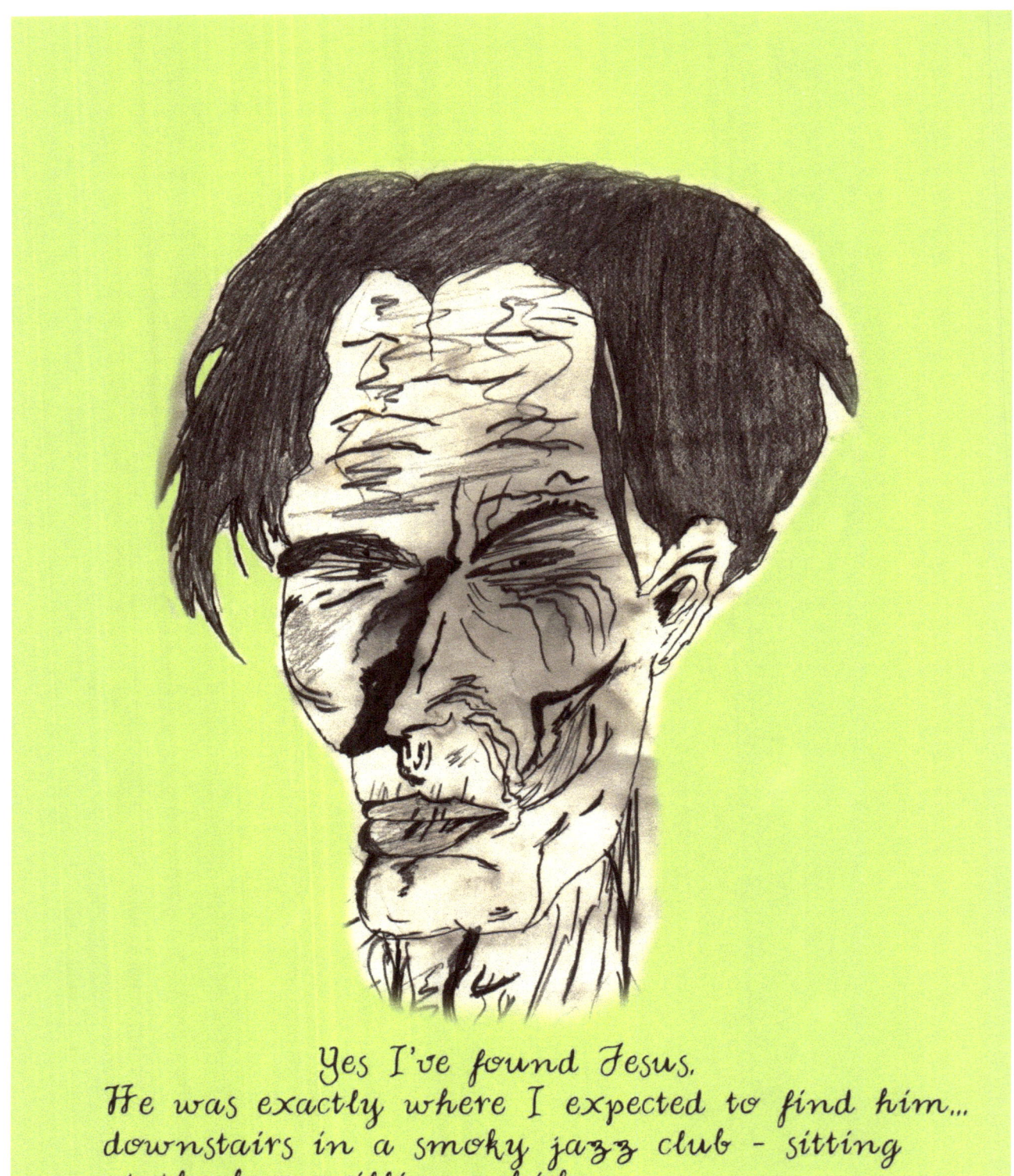

UNTITLED - (1982) mainly pencil

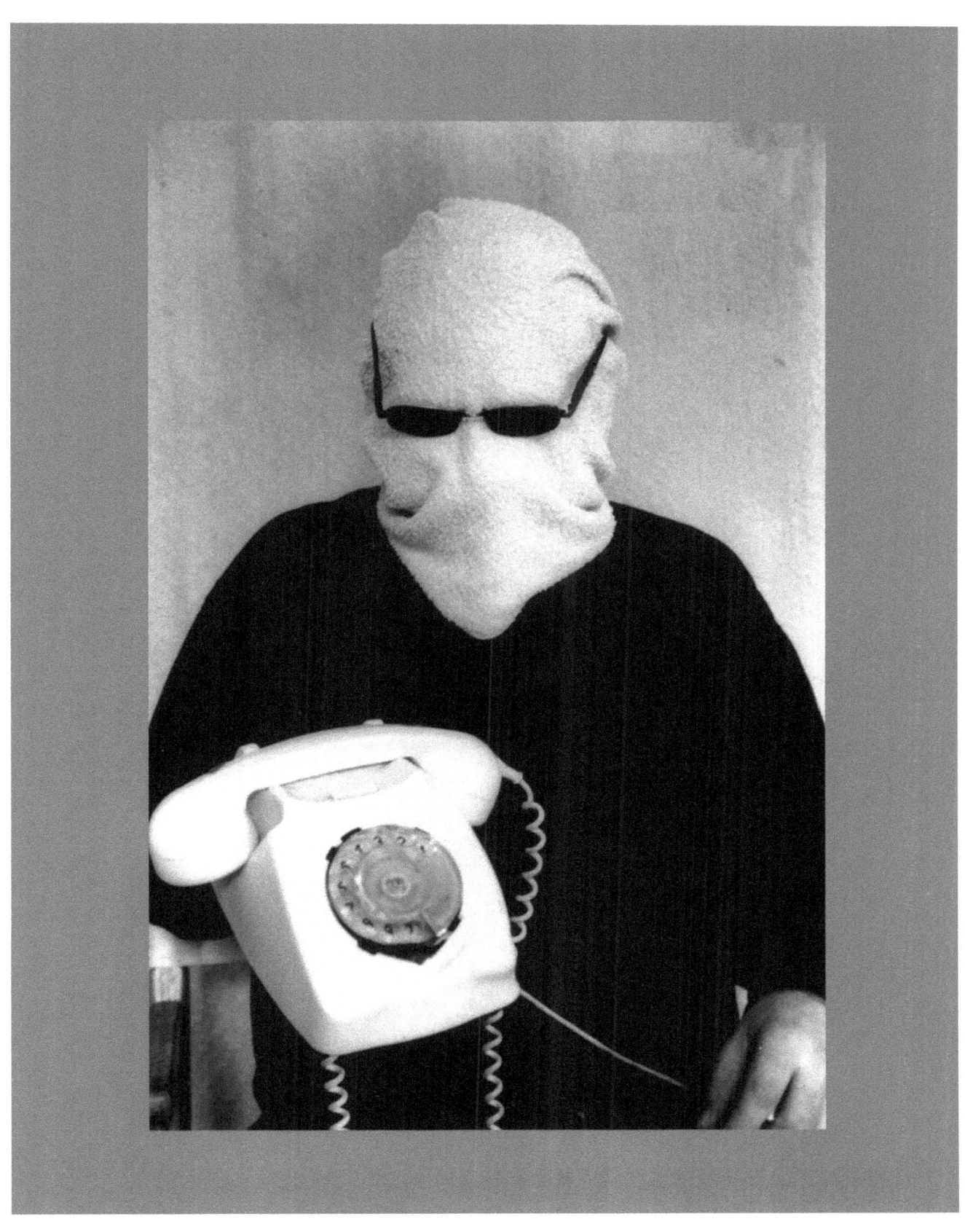

THAT TELEPHONE THING - (1999) photograph

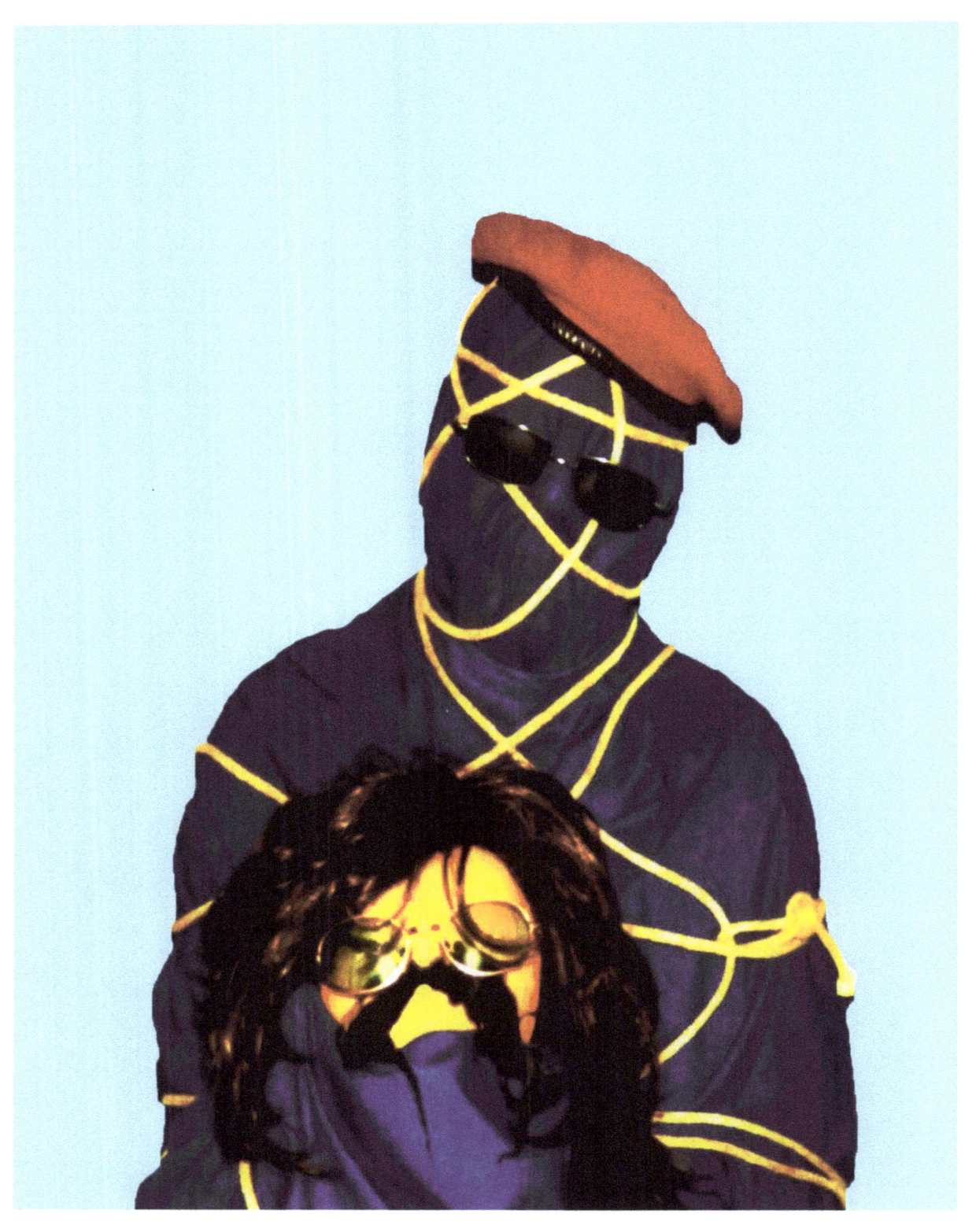

MEXICAN MELON TAKES MAN HOSTAGE - (2001)
photograph and slight treatments

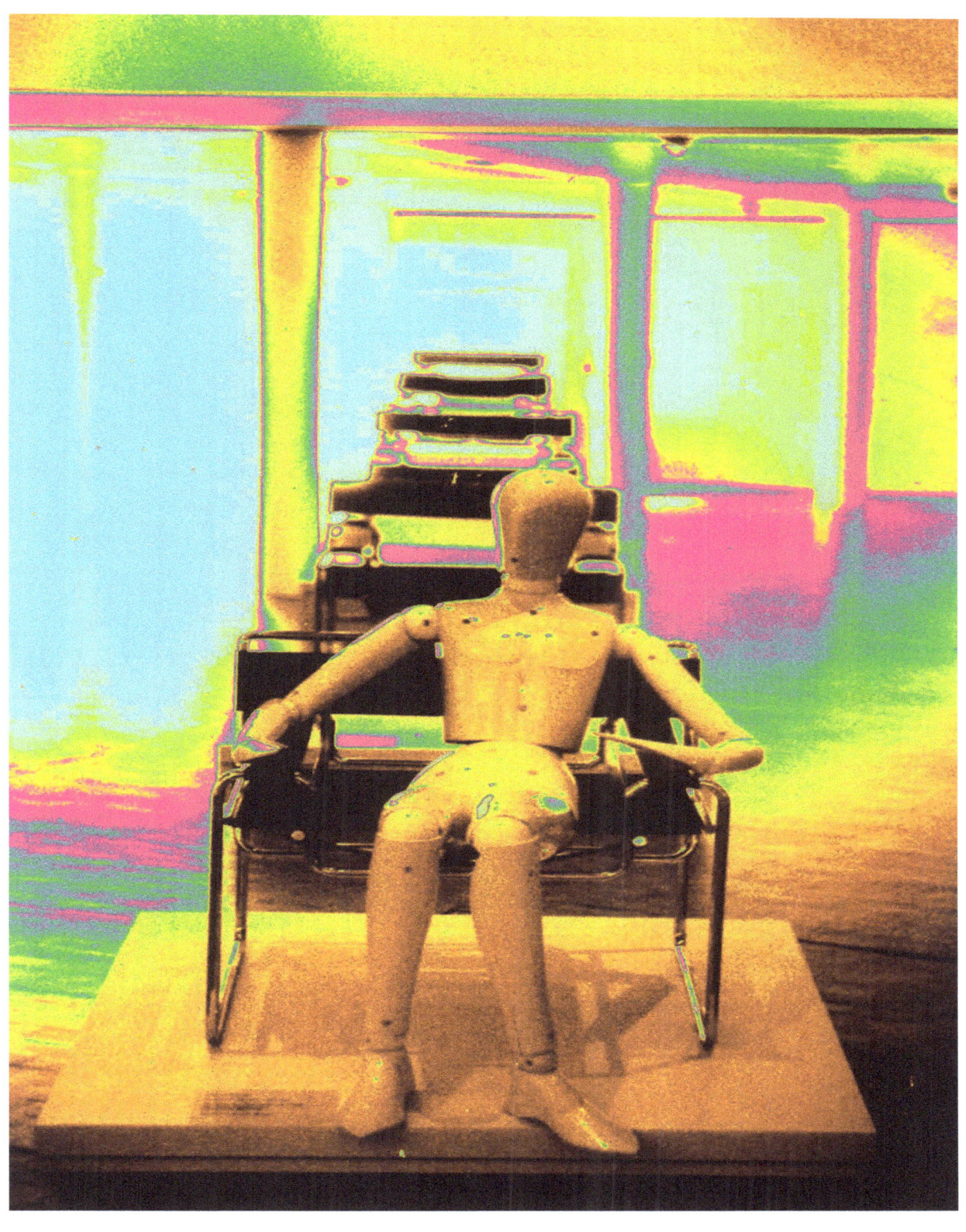

DUMMY-THINK - (1991) photograph and treatments

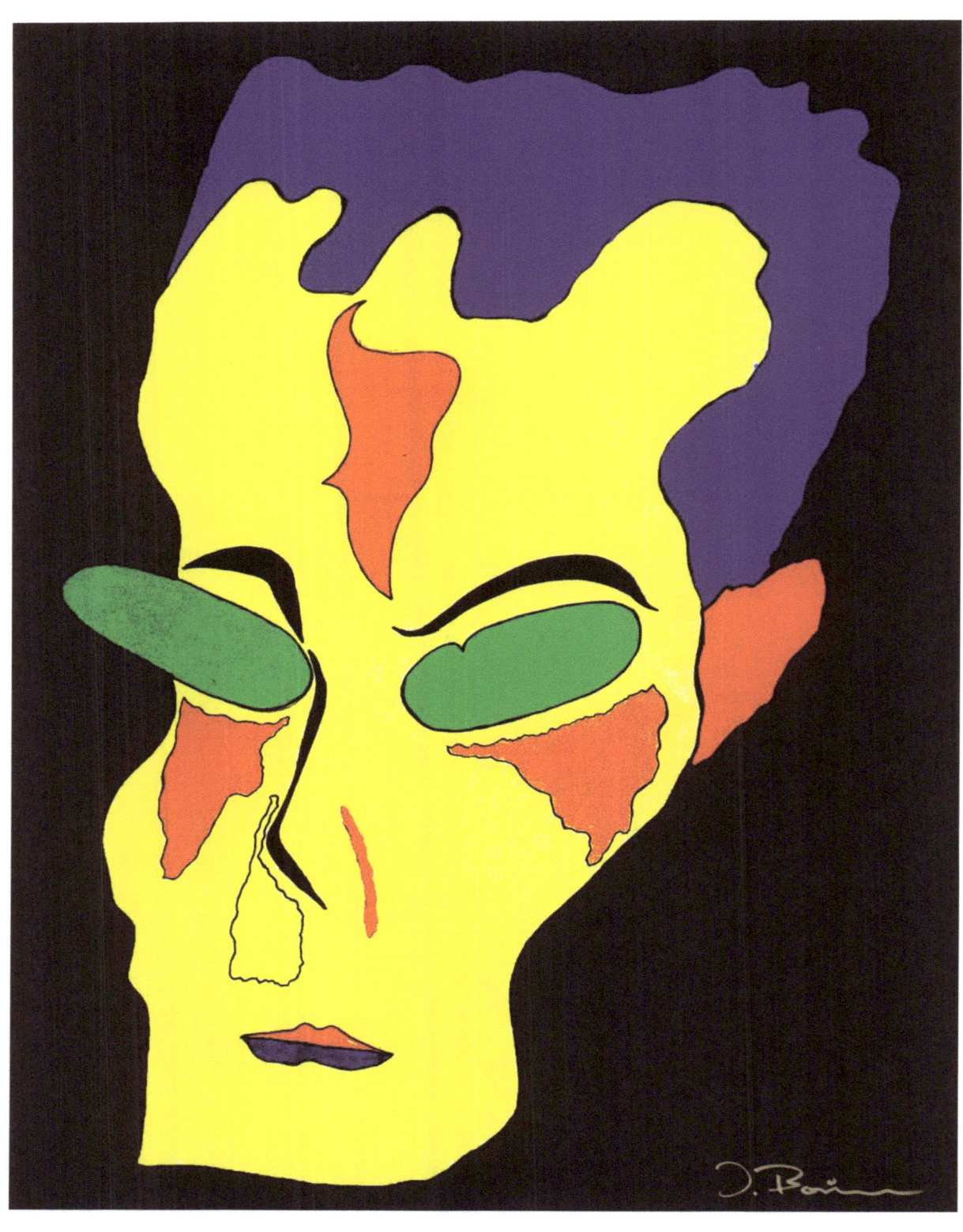

D-MAN - (1998) acrylic on board (mainly)

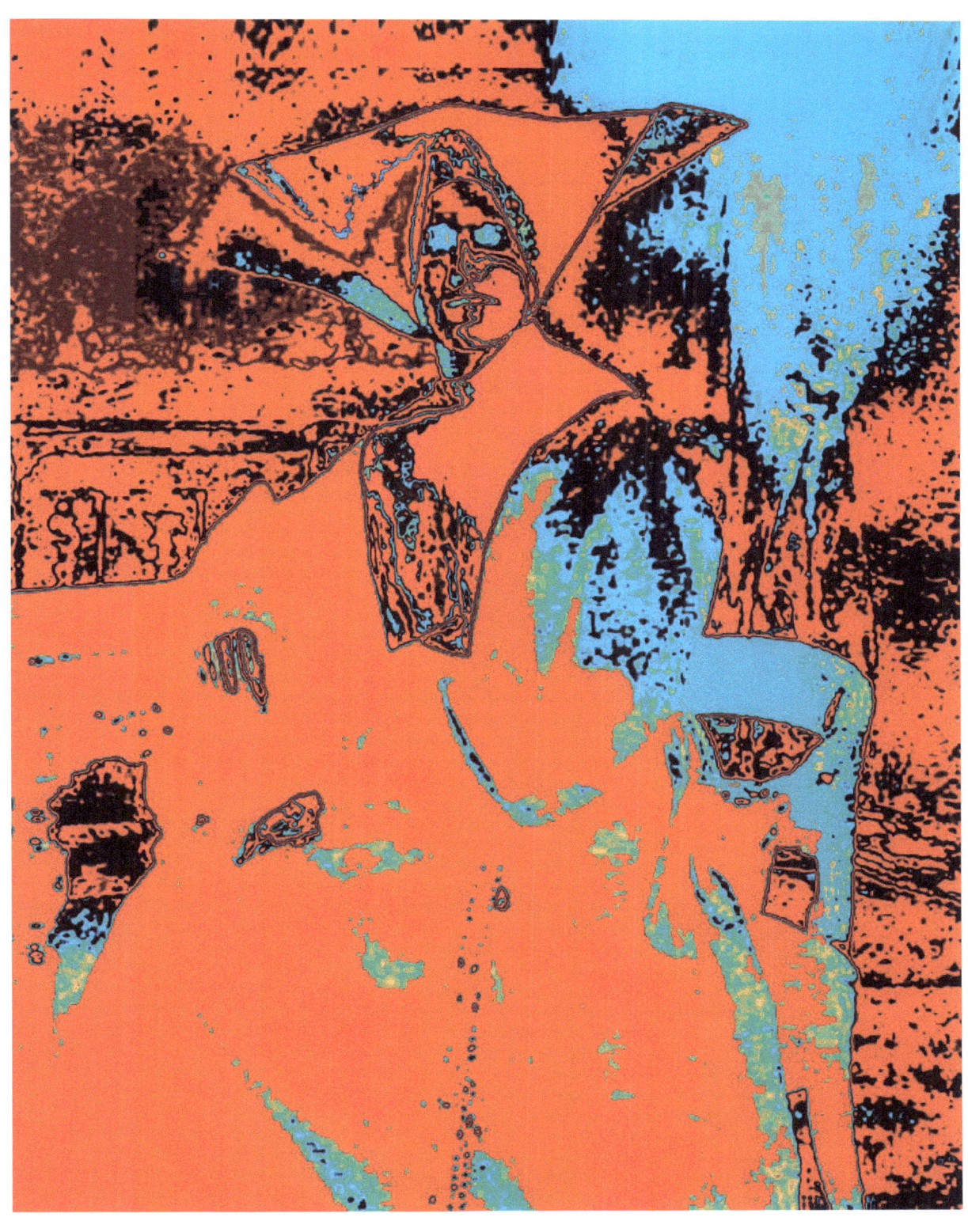

THE RED NUN - (2018) treated photograph

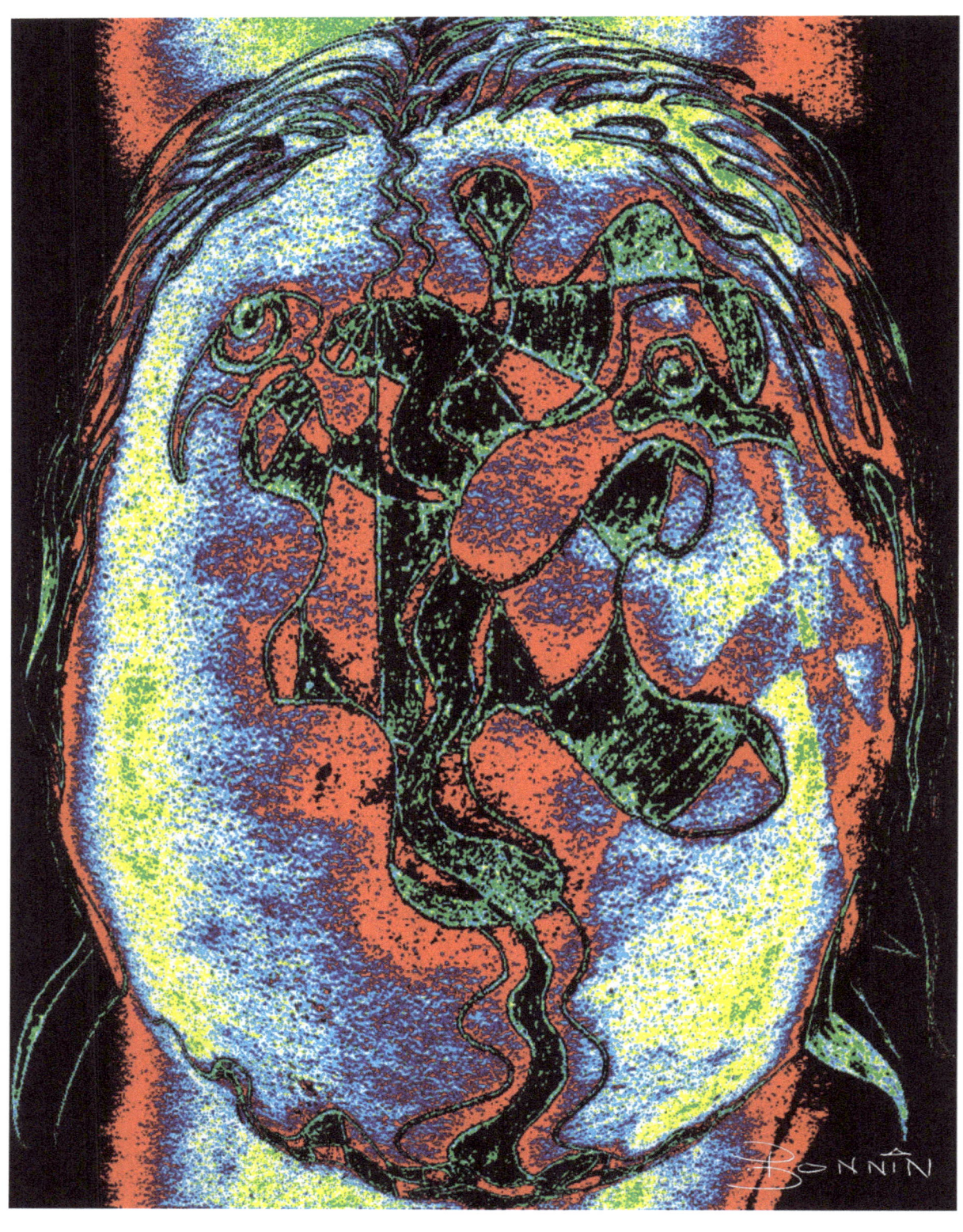

(OV POWER &) SELF PORTRAIT - (1984 AND 2016) pencil drawing photographed then painted then treated

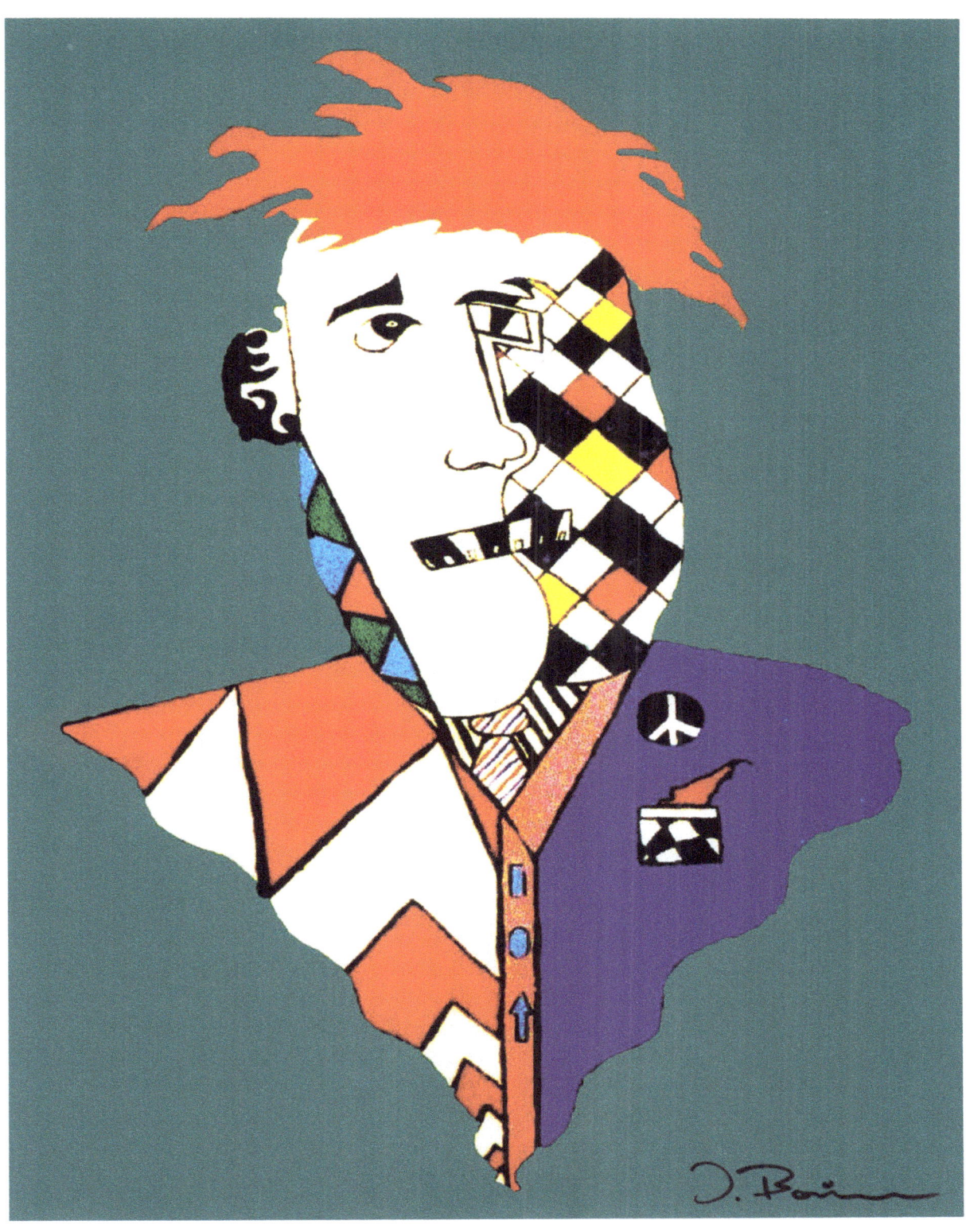

MUSIC MAN - (1984) acrylic on board then photographed in very sunny room, then slightly treated

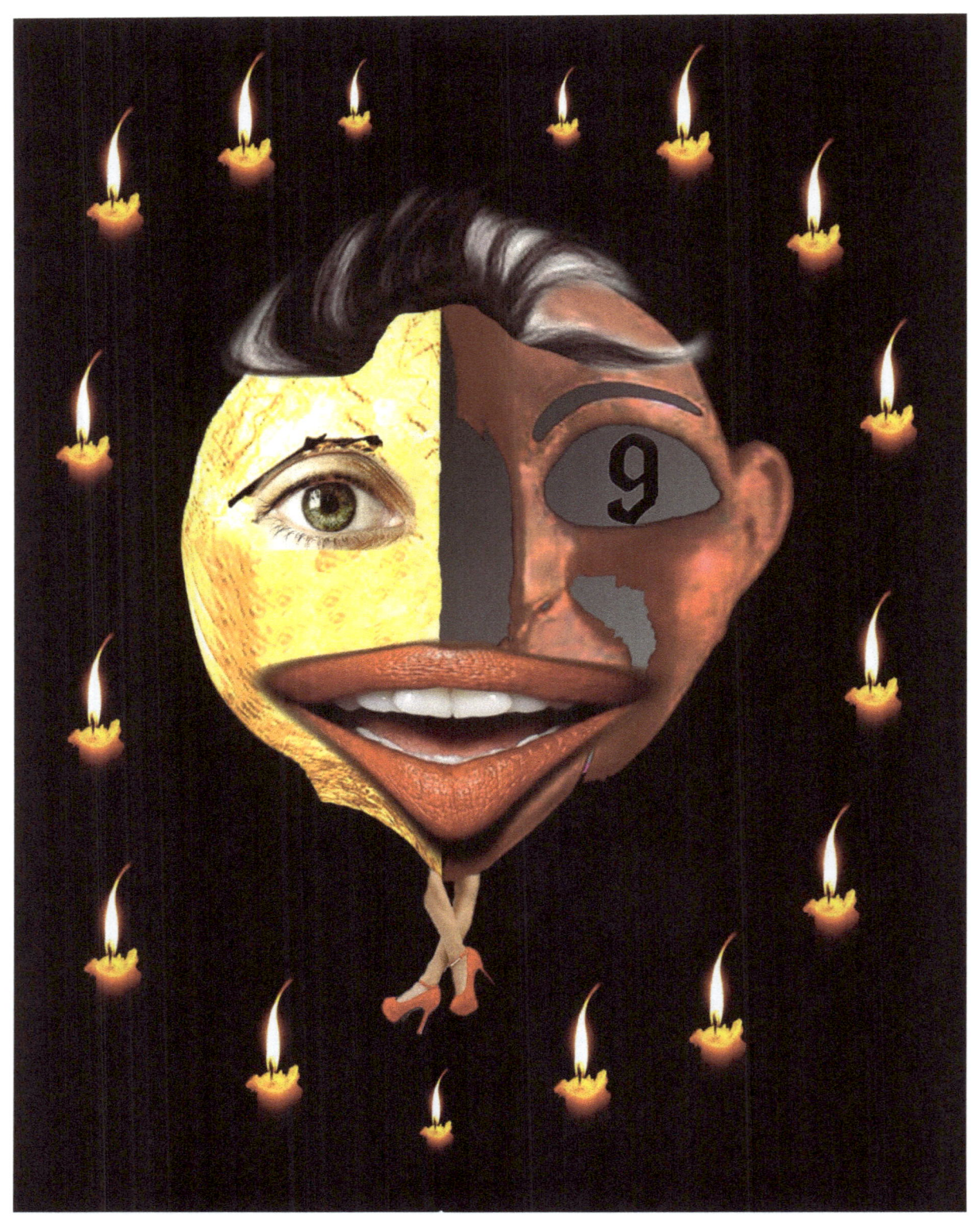

MR AND MS SAVANT-GARDE - (2018) collage and treatments

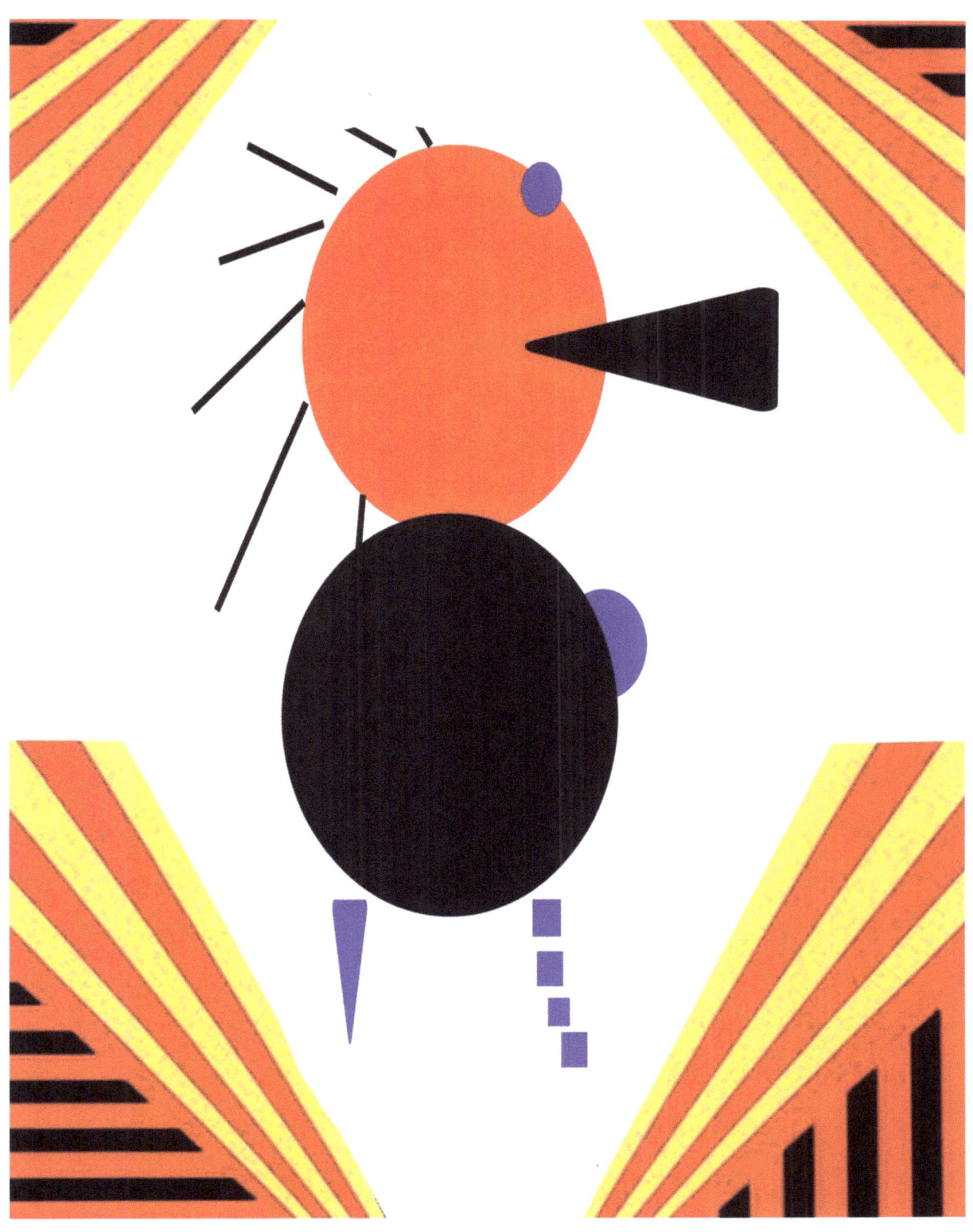

MS ABSTRACT - (2017) collage and treatments

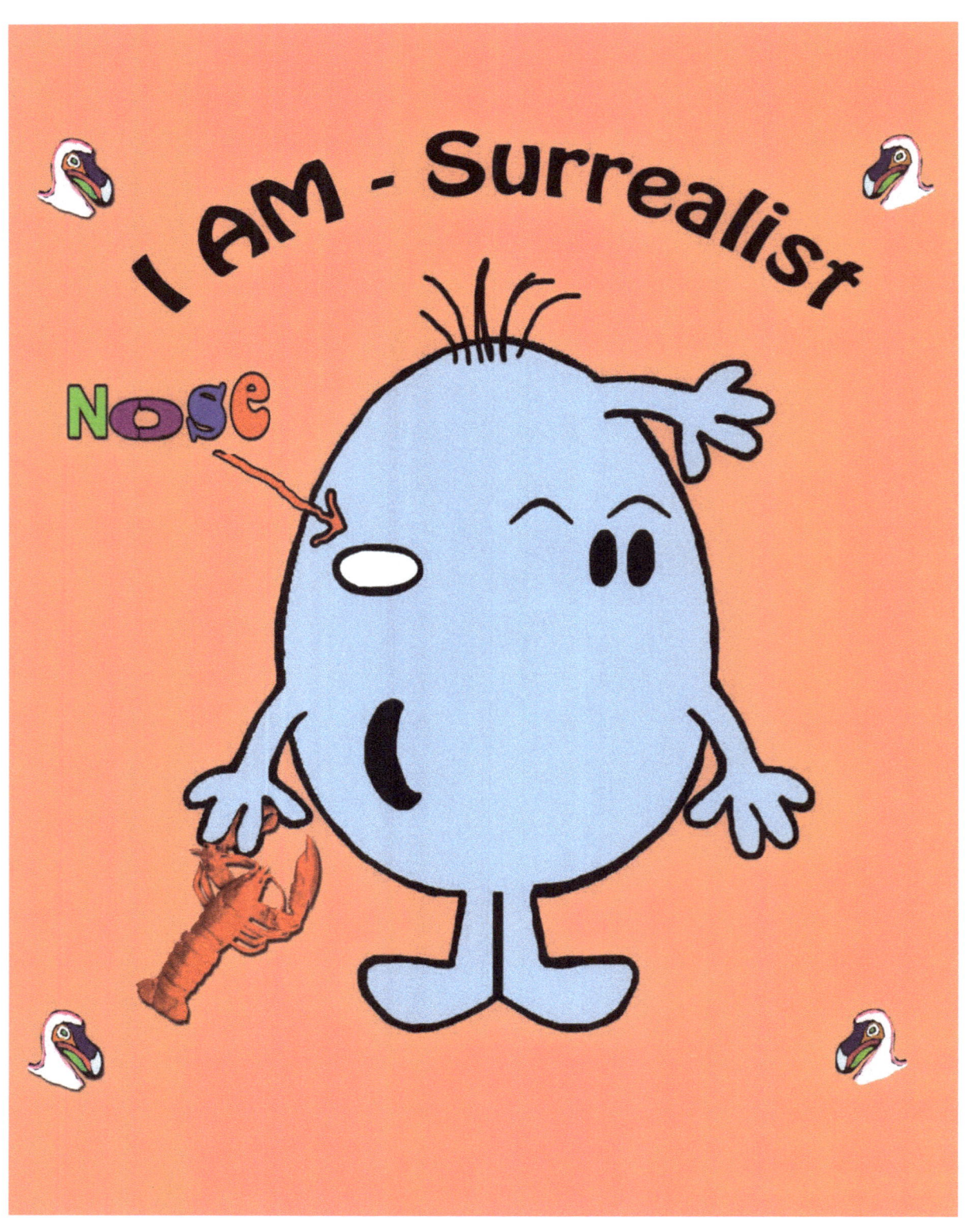

MR SURREALIST - (2017) collage and treatments

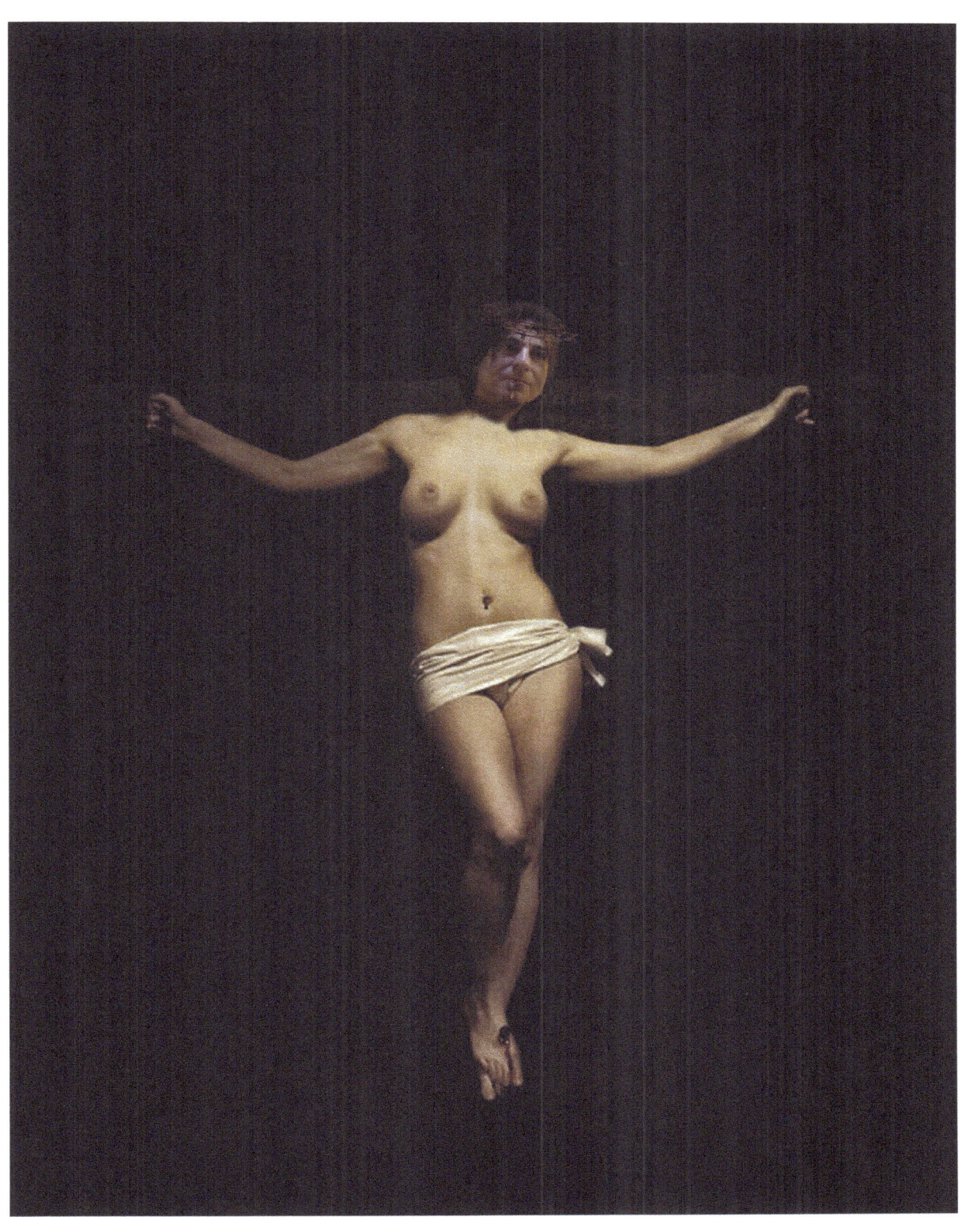

THE ANTI-JEAN - (2018) collage and treatments

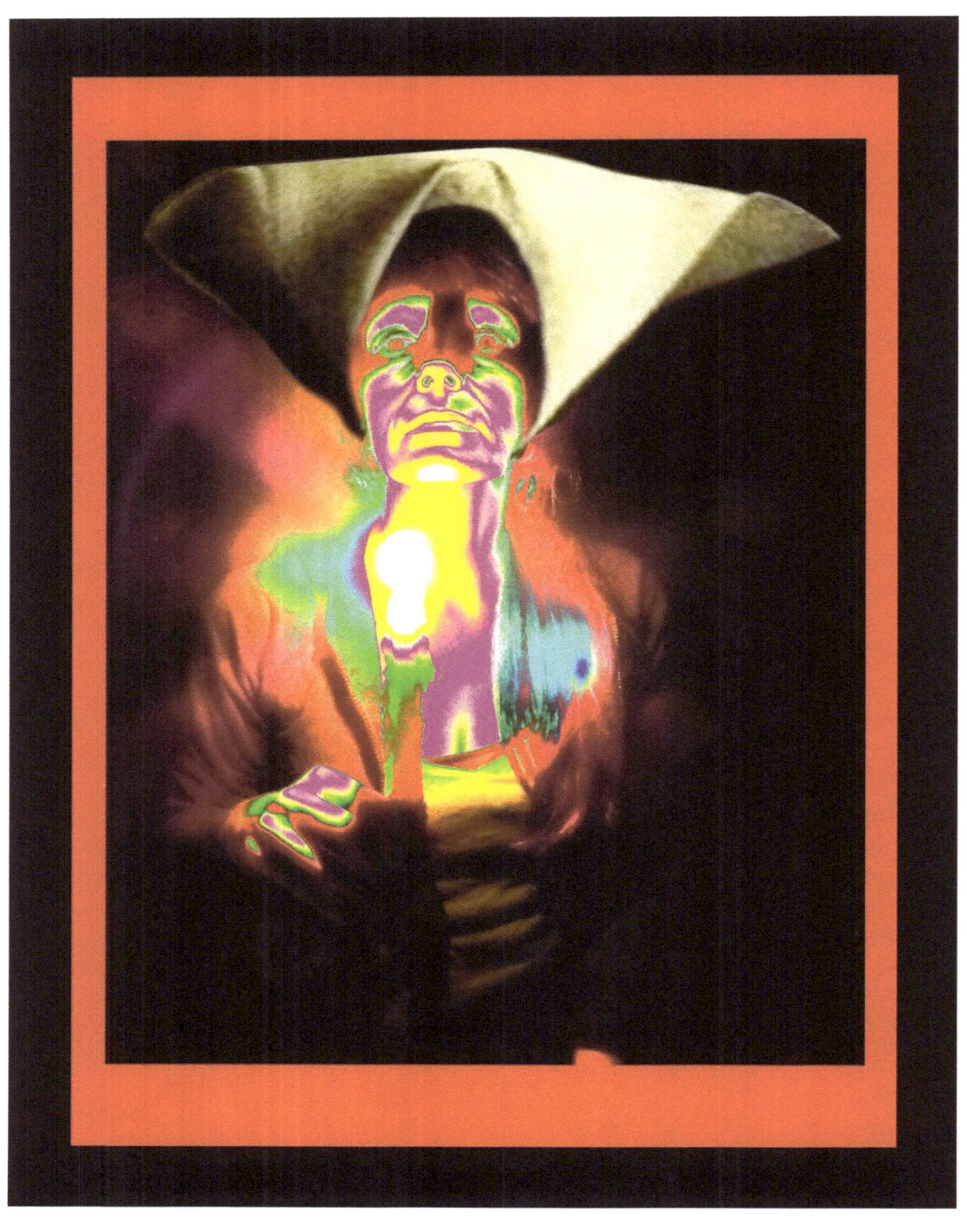

BURNING NUN - (2018) photograph and treatments

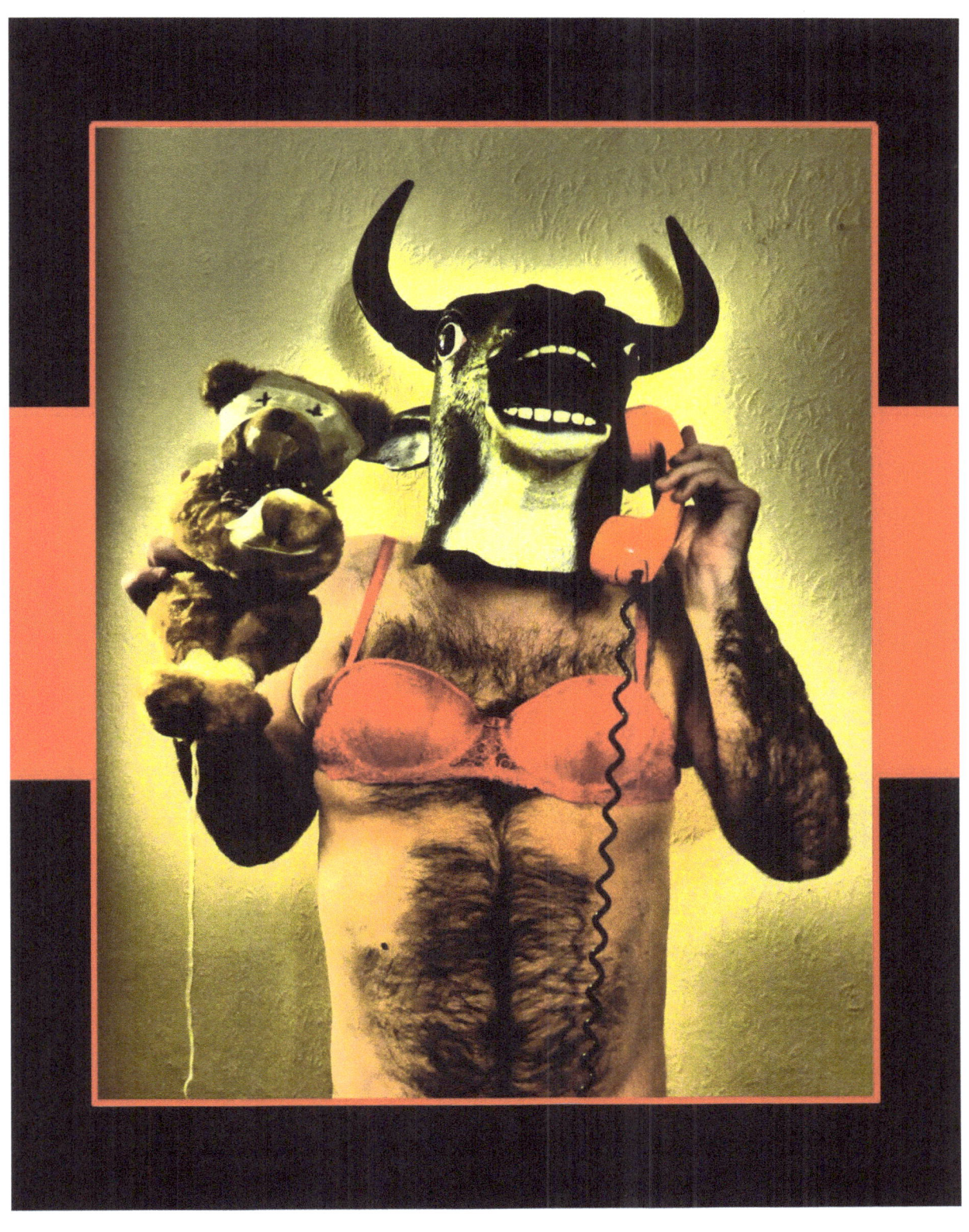

BEAR HOSTAGE - (2016-2017) photograph and treatments

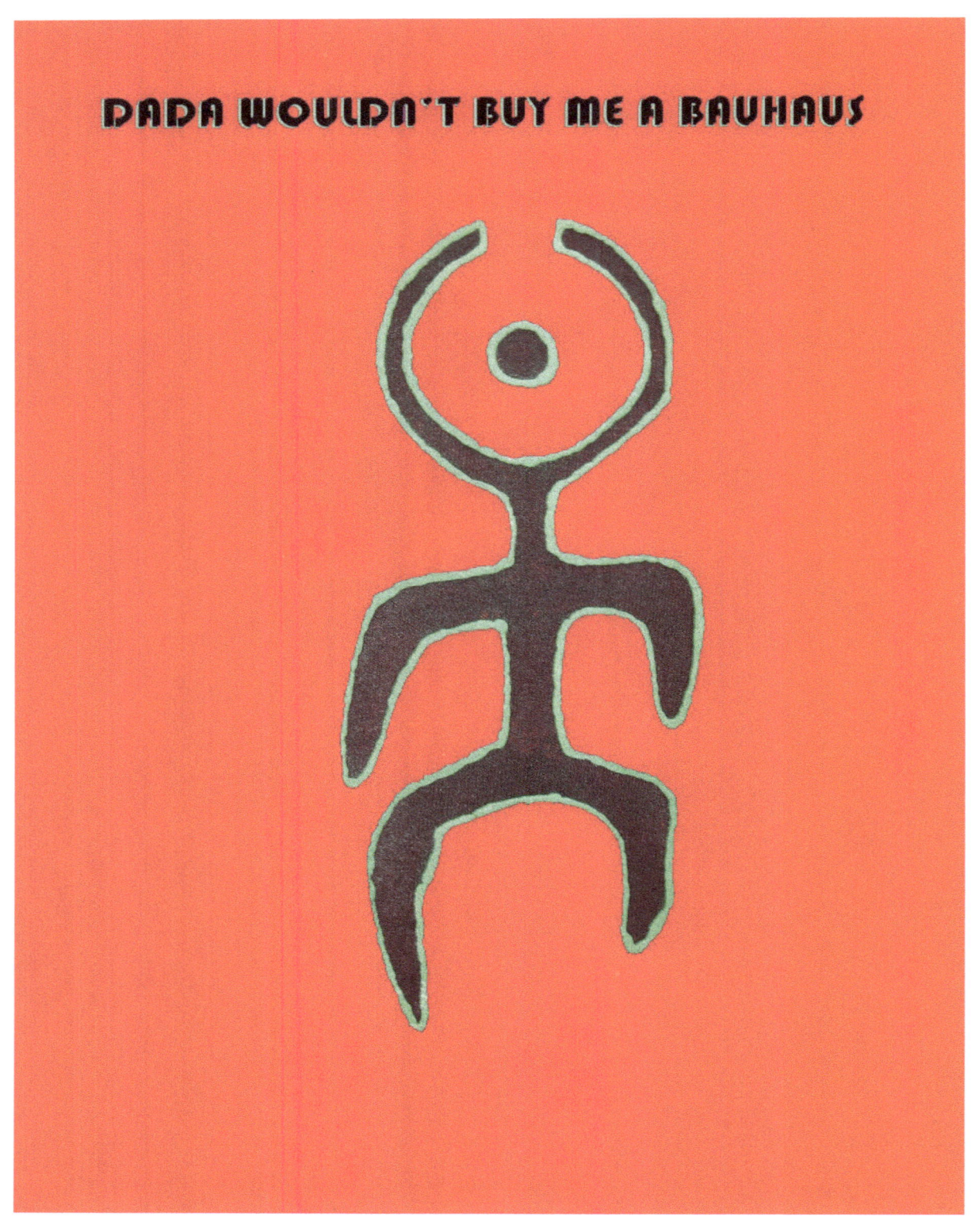

DADA ALIEN - (circa **2000**) initially an acrylic painting, subsequently slightly treated

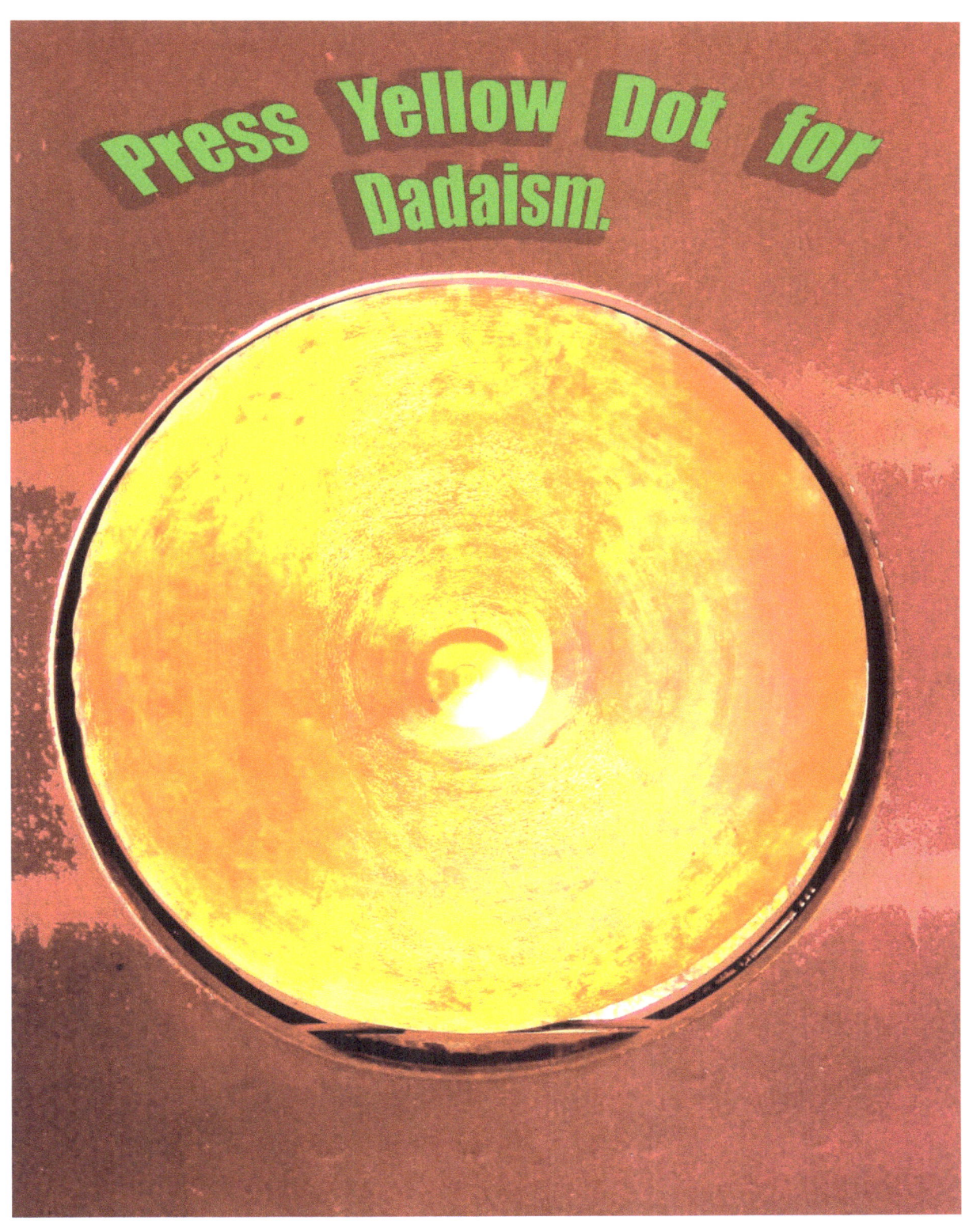

DADA DOT - (circa 1999) Mexican photo treated

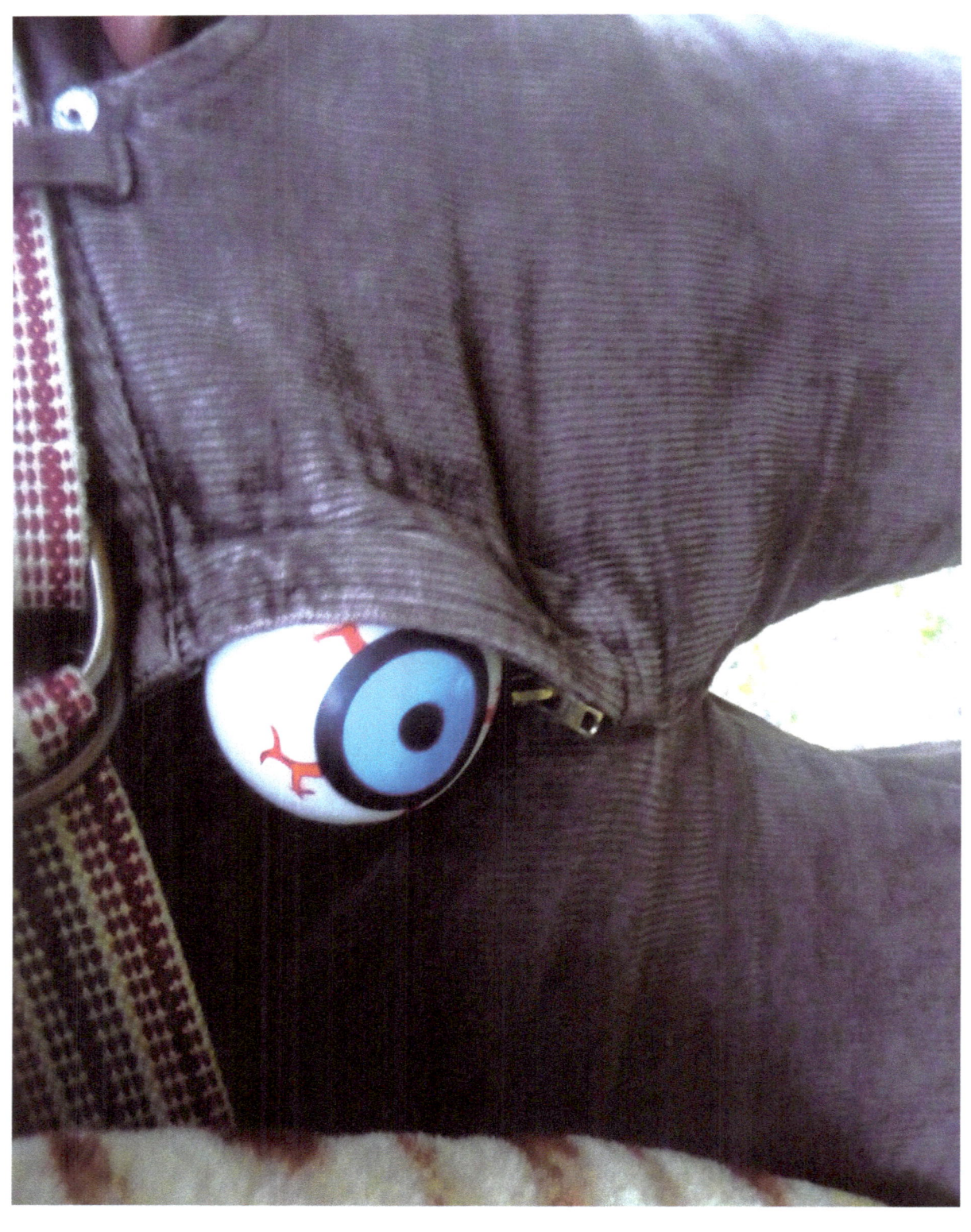

I WAS GOING TO CALL THIS 'COCKEYED' BUT I DIDN'T HAVE THE BALLS - (2016) photograph

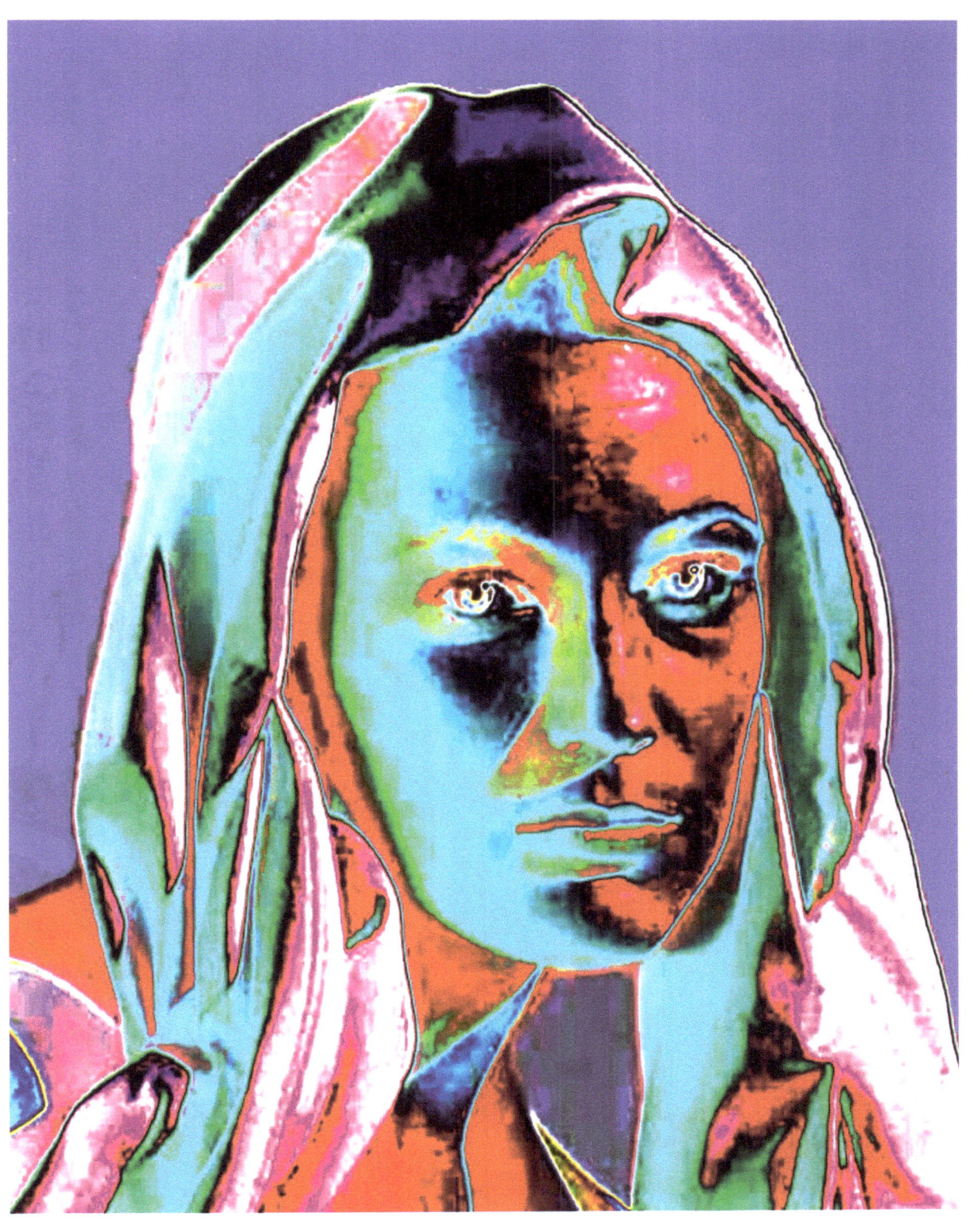

CUBIST MARY - (2018) treatments

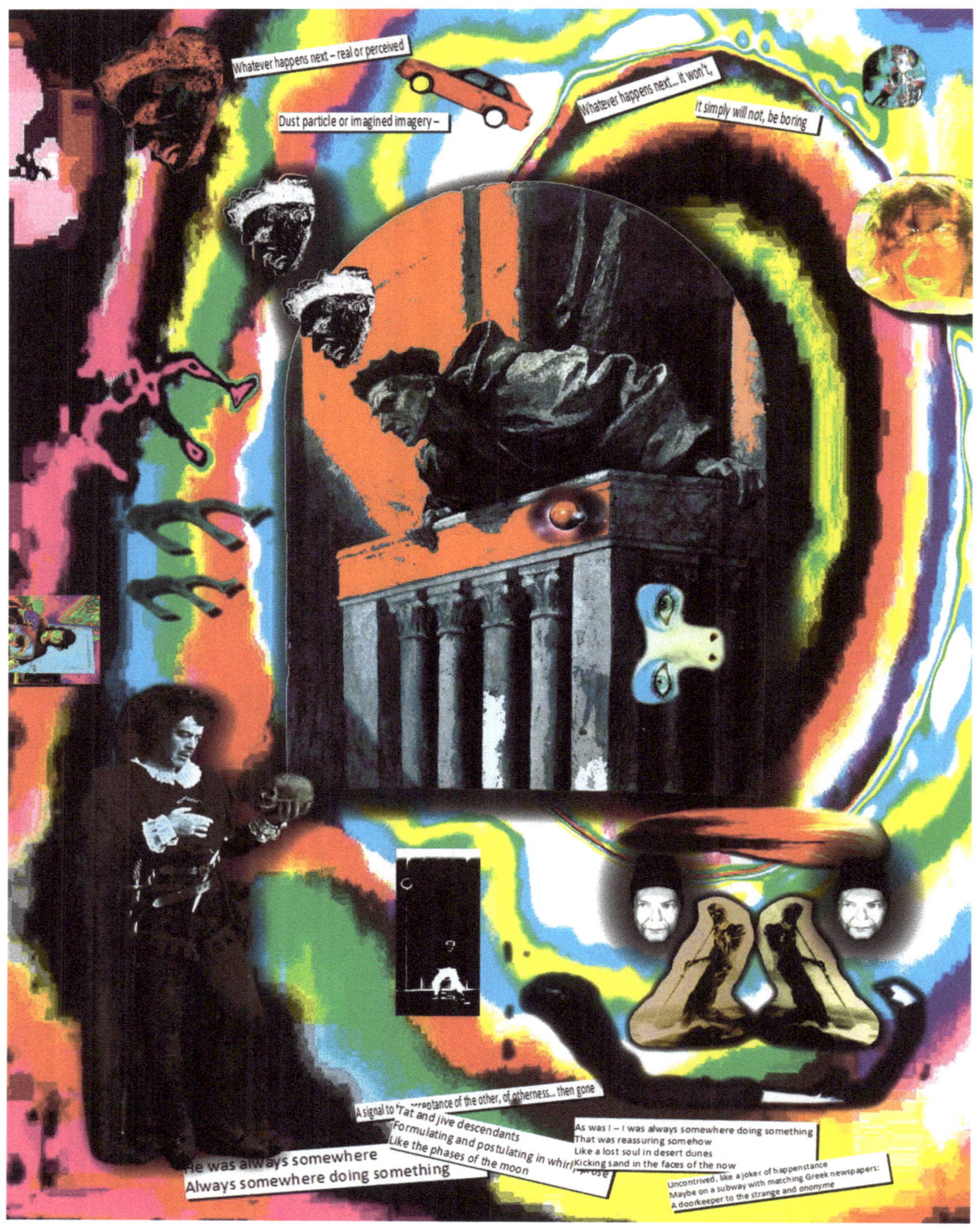

THE WILLED RESURRECTION OF DAVID JONES
(IN HOMAGE TO DAVID BOWIE) - (2016) collage mainly, plus treatments

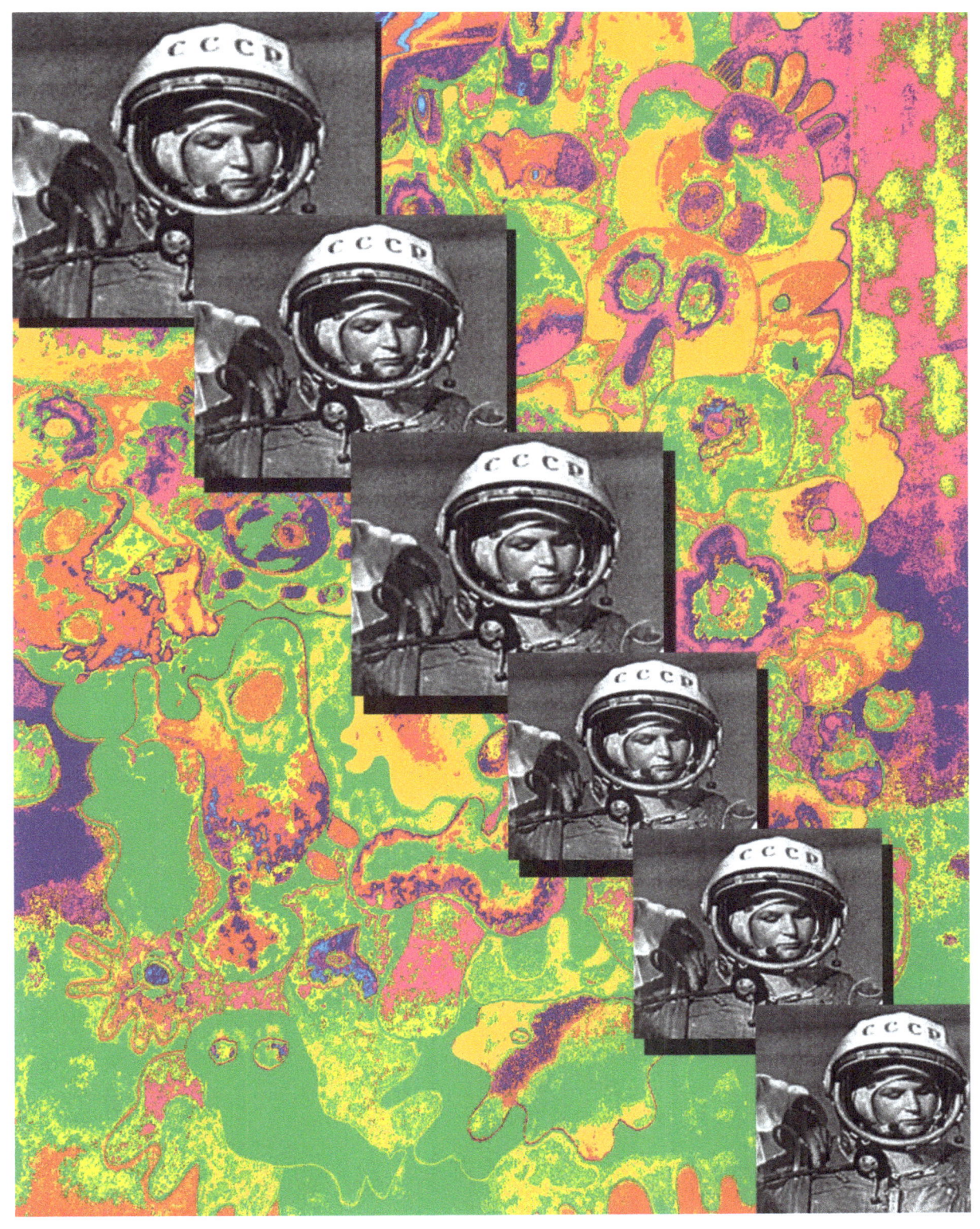

VALENTINA TERESHKOVA (THE FIRST WOMAN IN SPACE) - (CIRCA **2002**) cut-out photograph/picture stuck onto board, photographed and treated

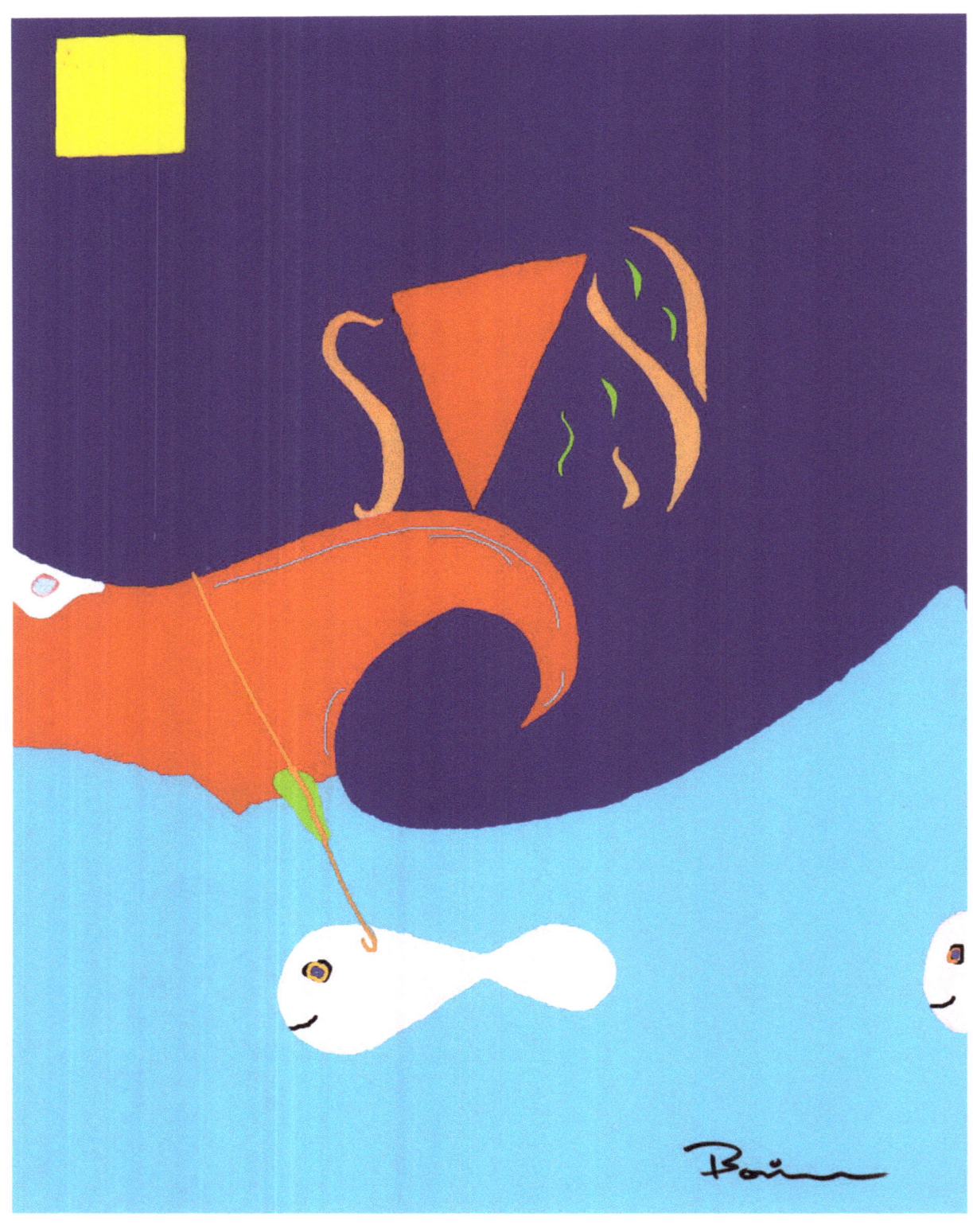

SEA & FISH II - (CIRCA 1986) acrylic on board mainly

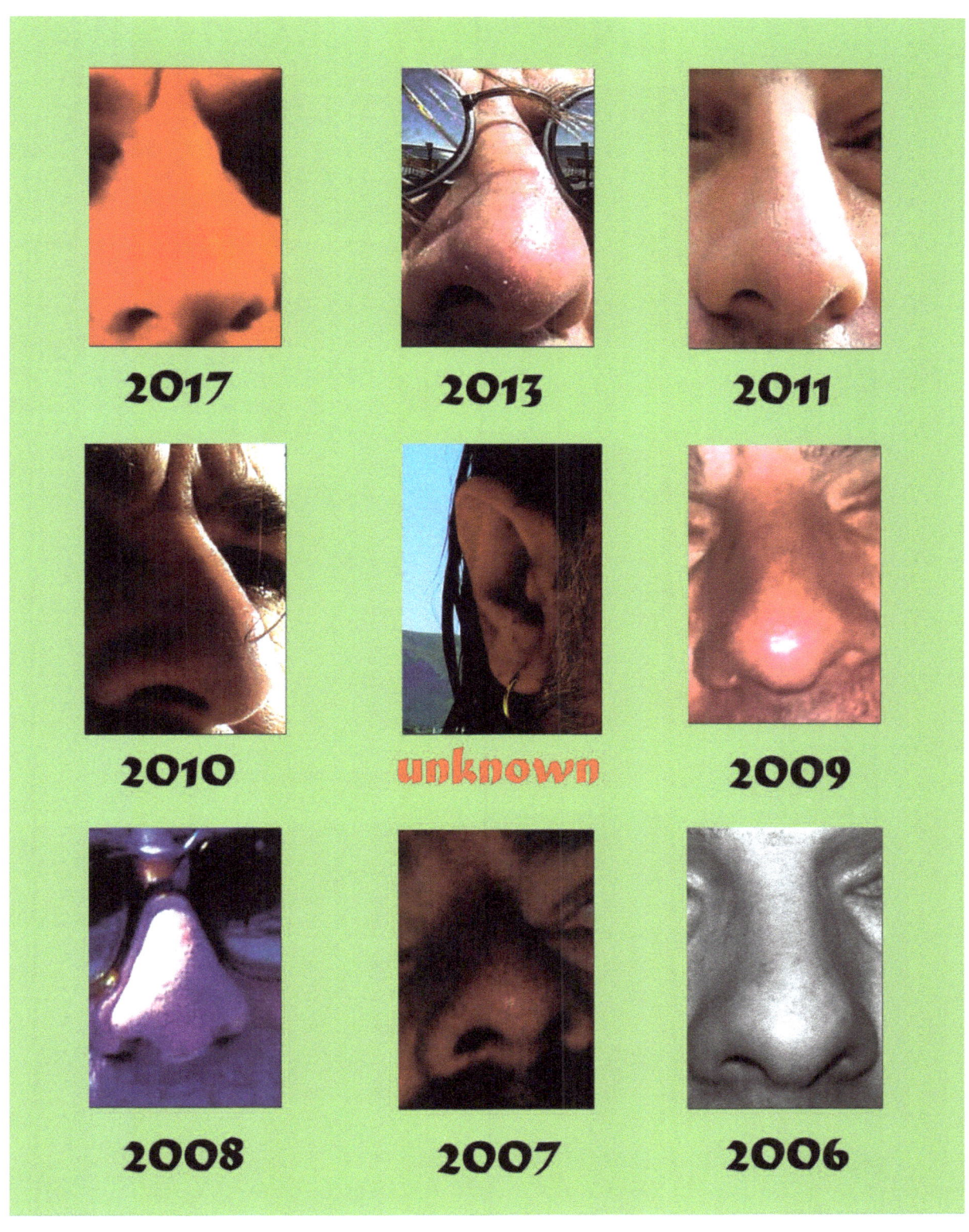

NO ONE NOSE - (2017) photographs and treatments

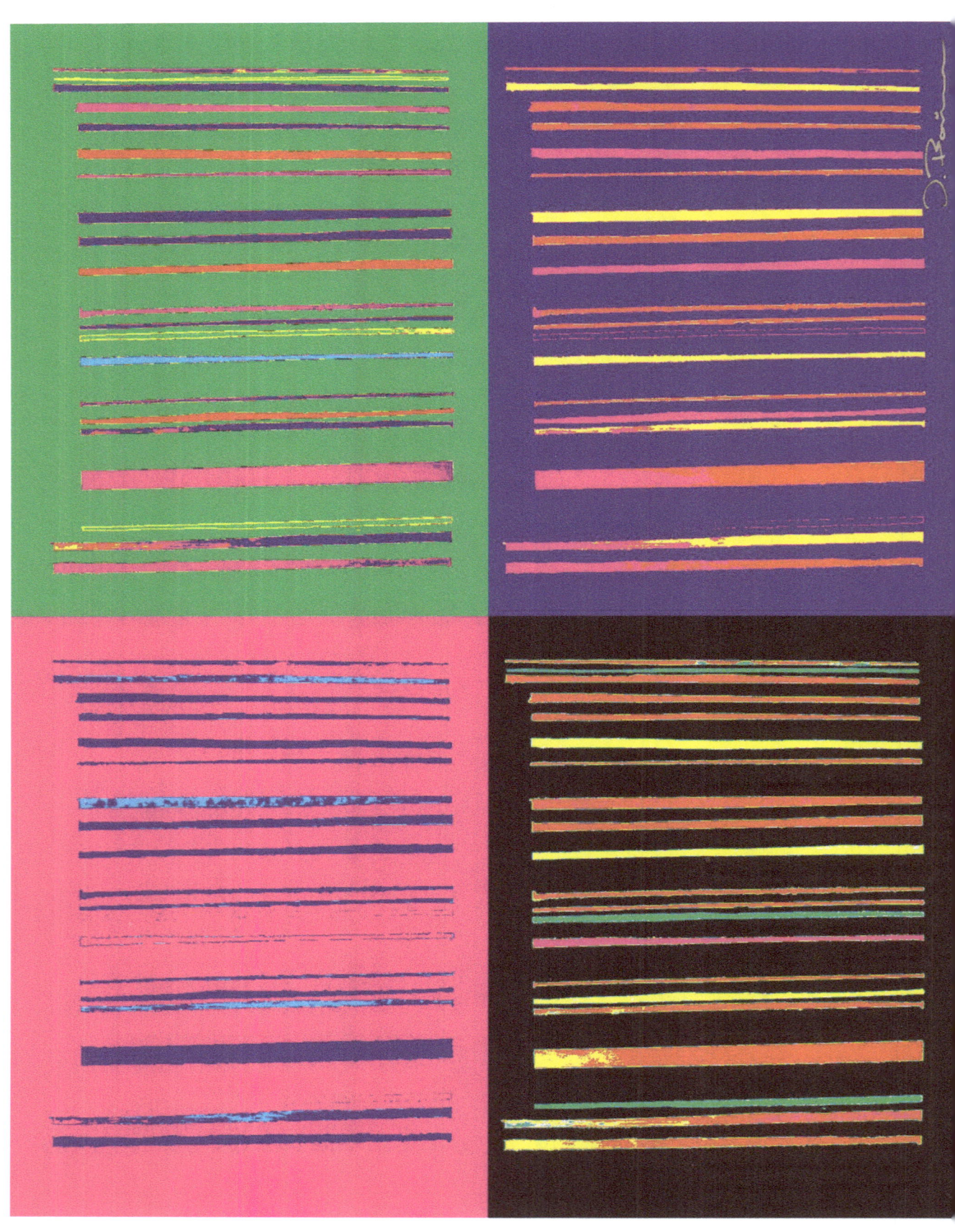

LINES V - (2001) acrylic on board with slight treatments

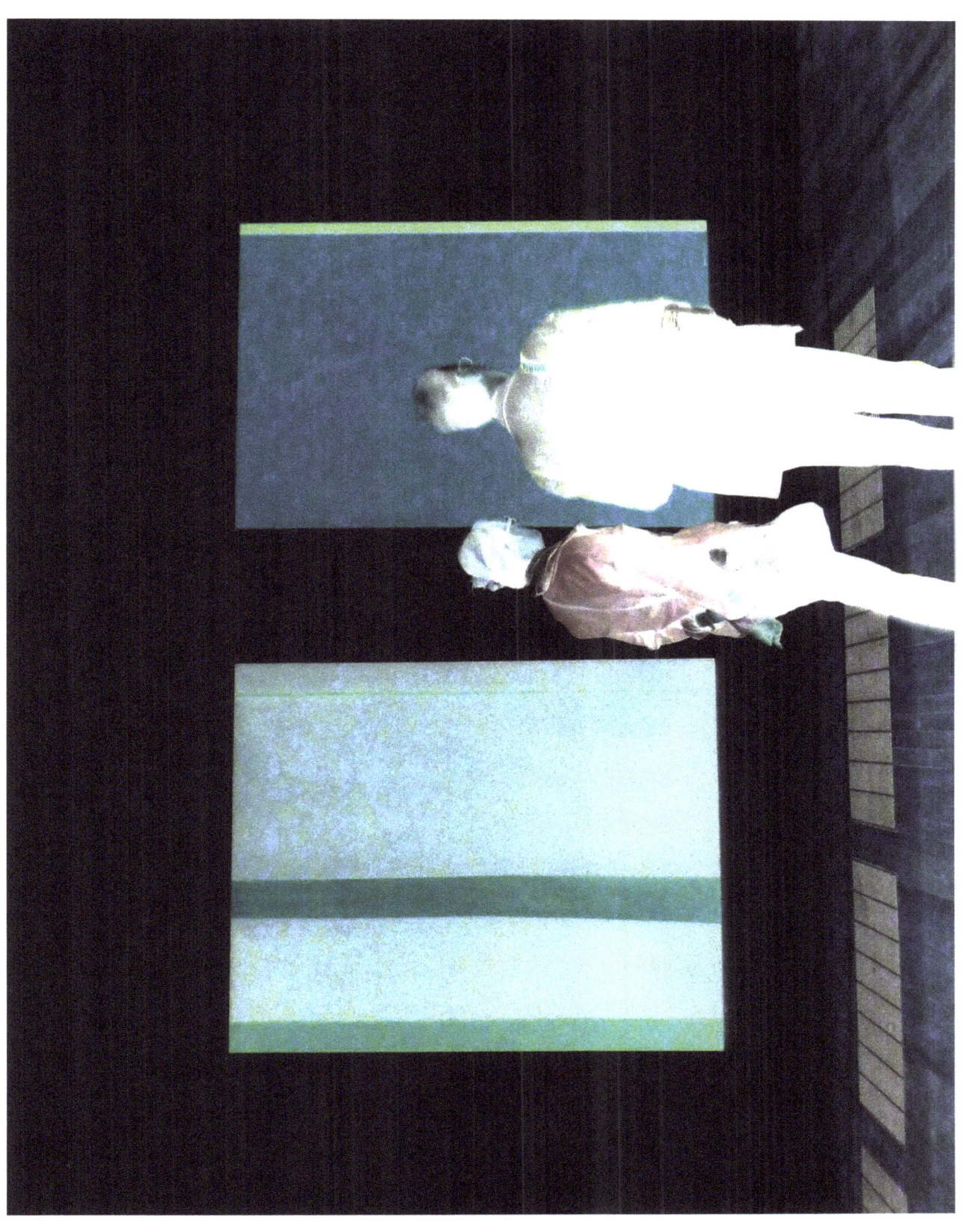

KILLER COUPLE CONSIDERING ART - (2008) photograph with treatments

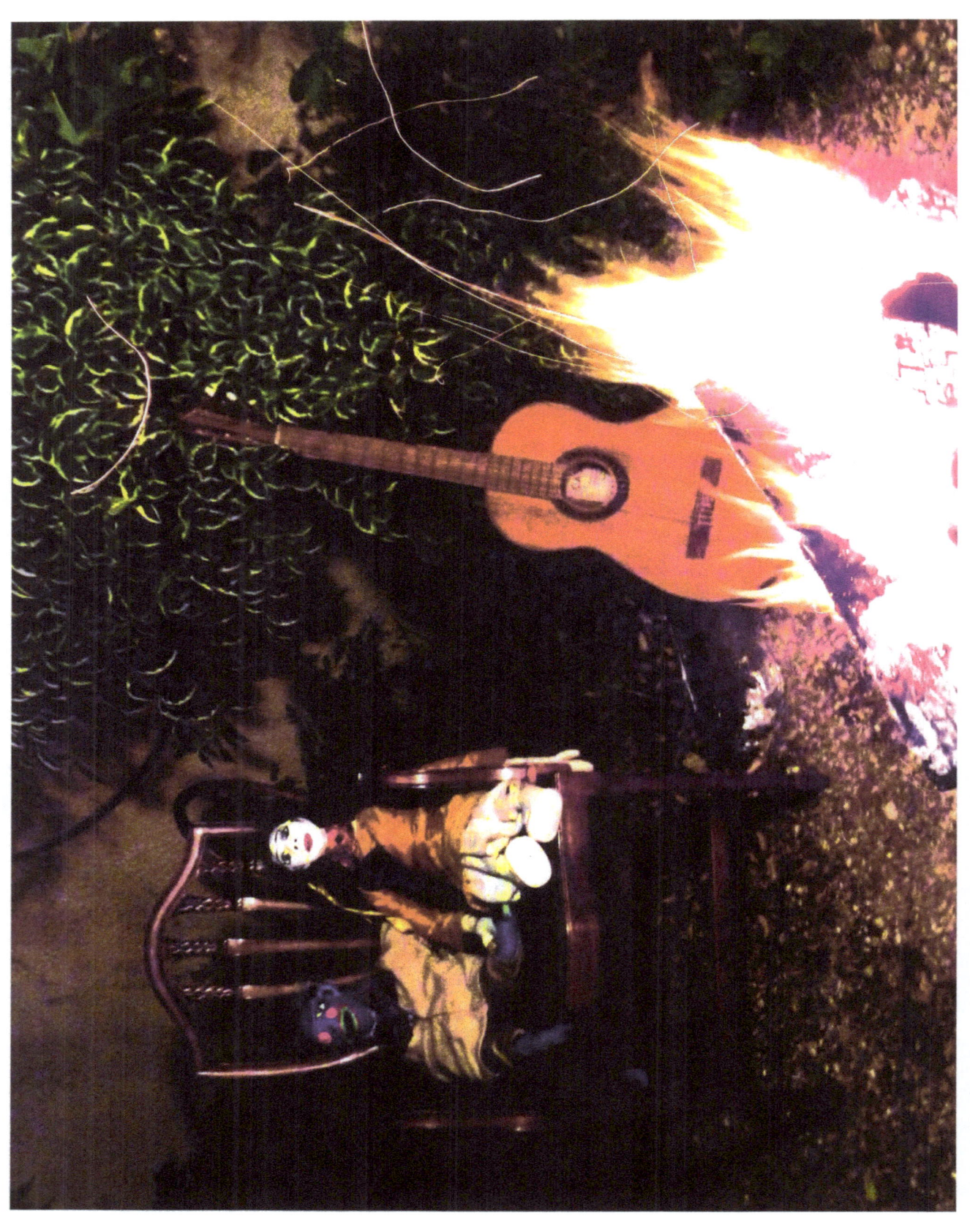

FIRE PUPPETS - (2015) photograph with treatments

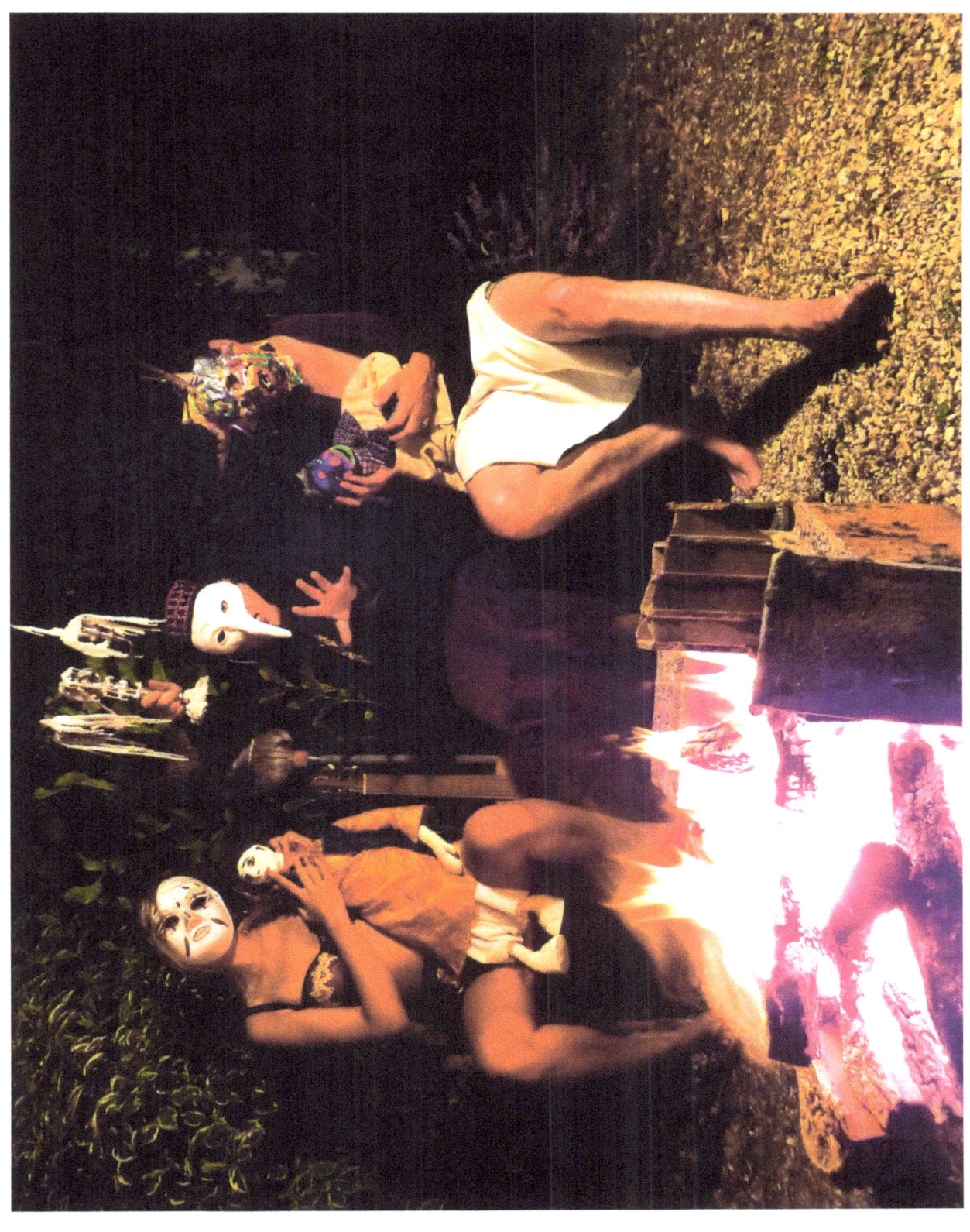

FIRE MONSTERS II - (2015) photograph with treatments

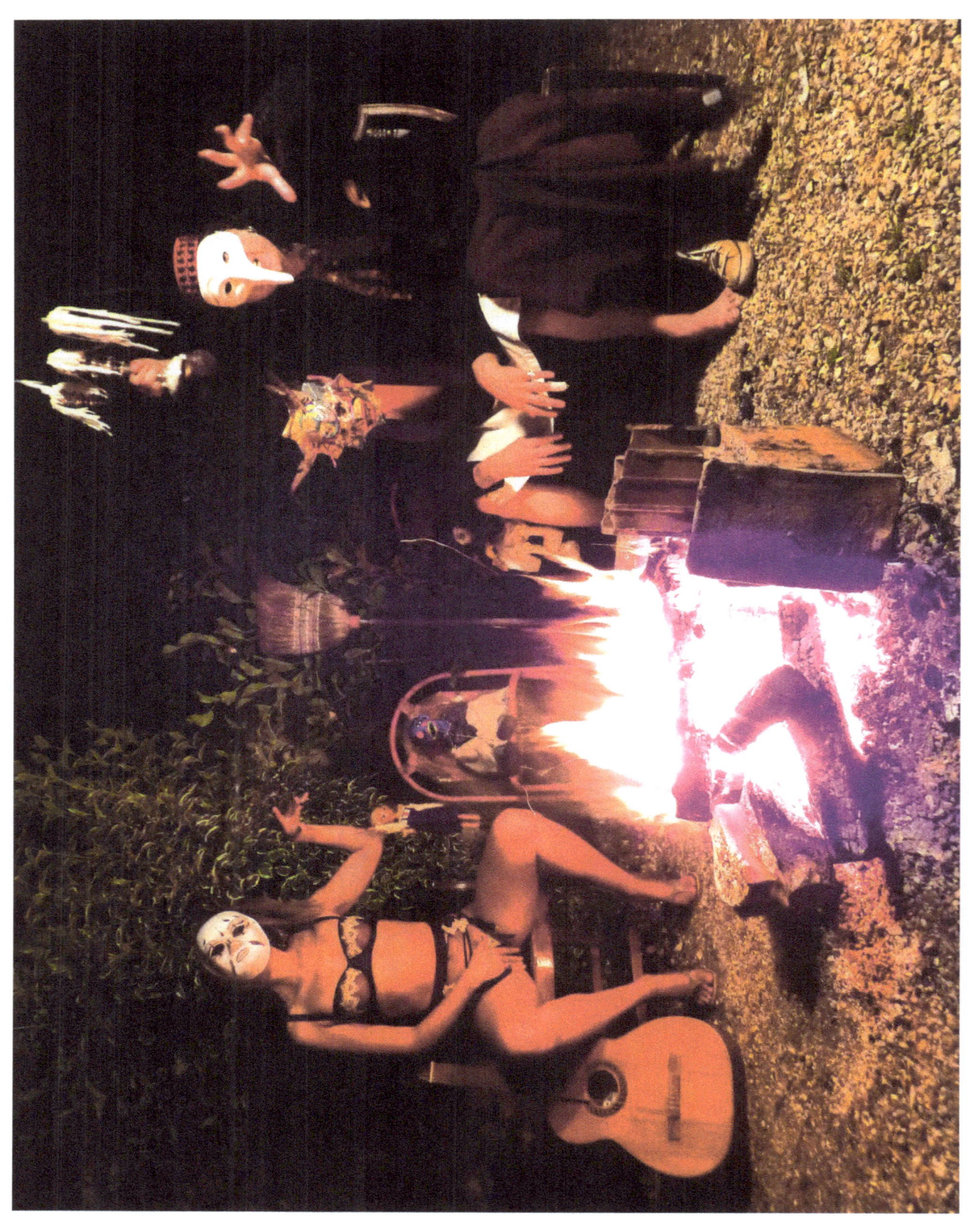

FIRE MONSTERS - (2015) photograph and treatments

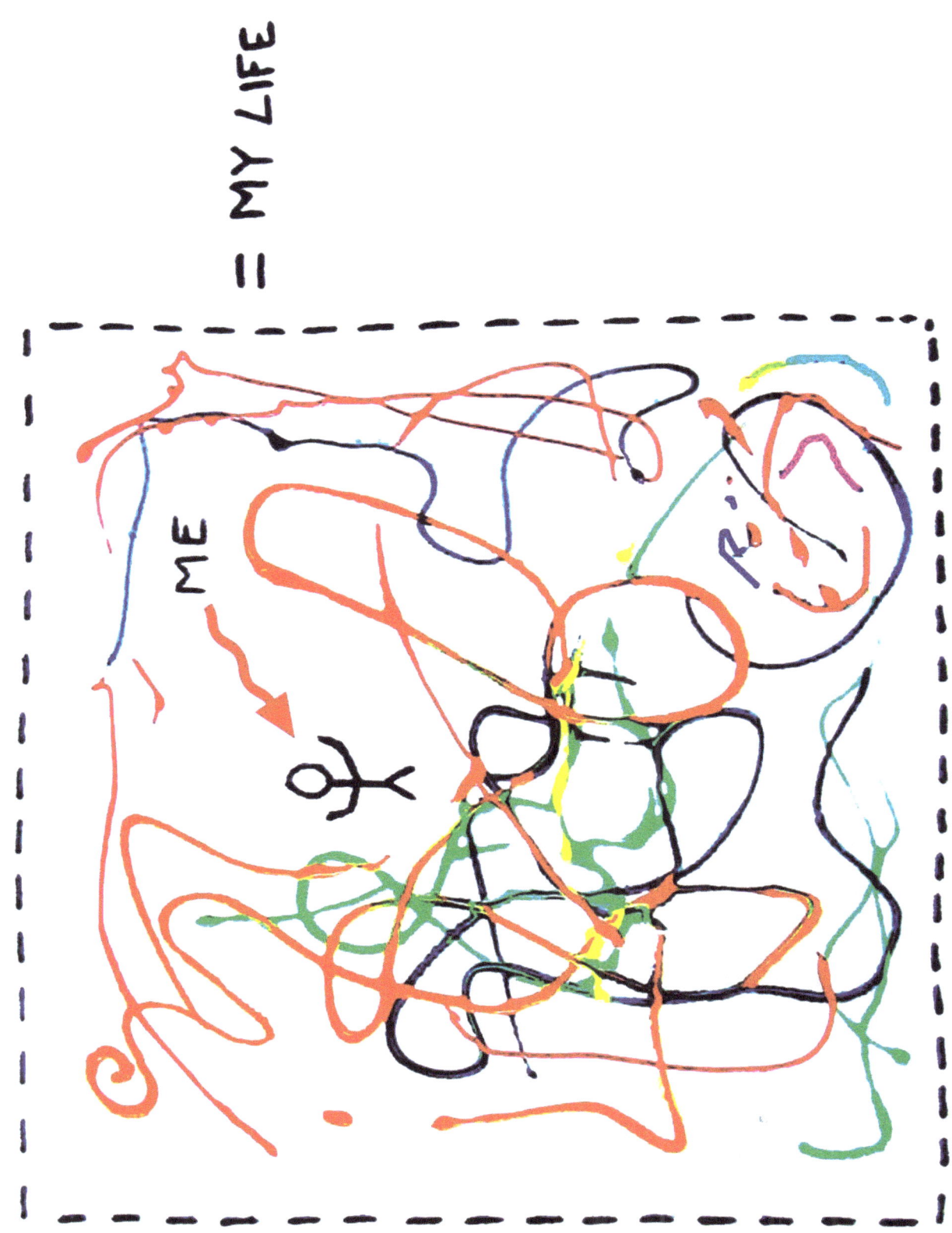

MY LIFE - (CIRCA **2001**) acrylic on board (mainly)

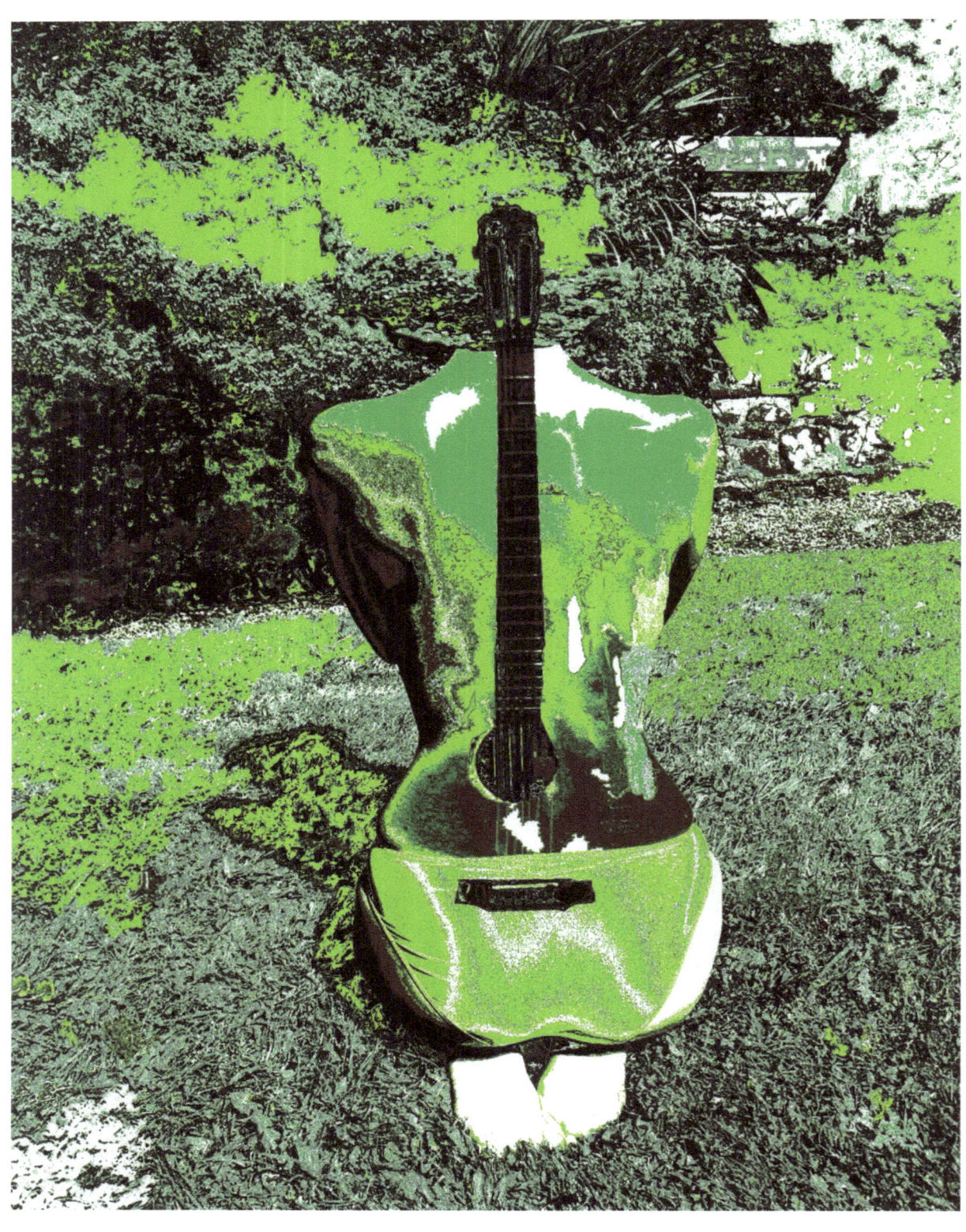

GUITAR (GREEN) - (2016) photograph with treatments

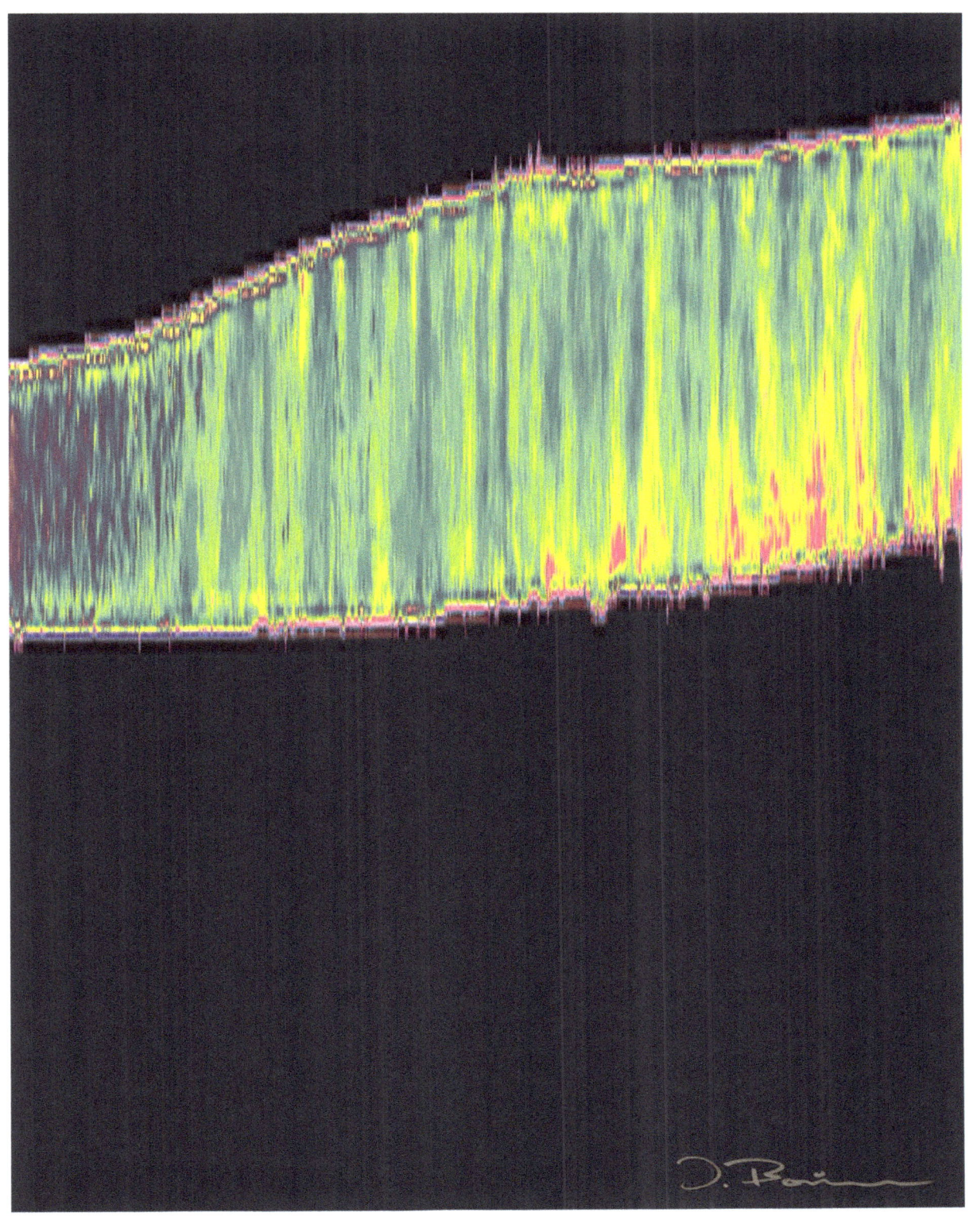

GREEN ELECTRIQUE - (UNDATED) photographed sound then treated

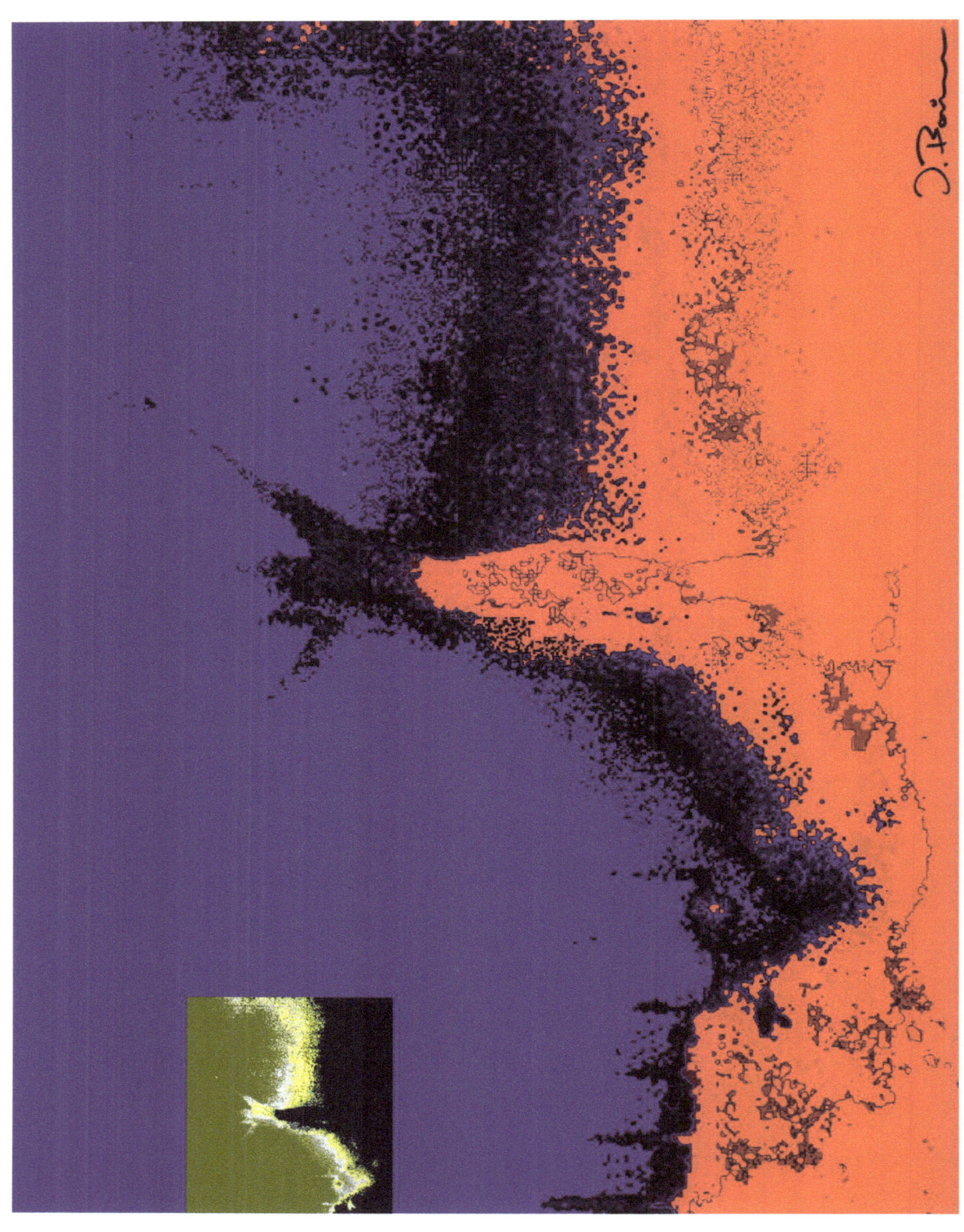

EXPLODING THE MYTHS - (UNDATED) photograph and acrylic paint, photographed with treatments

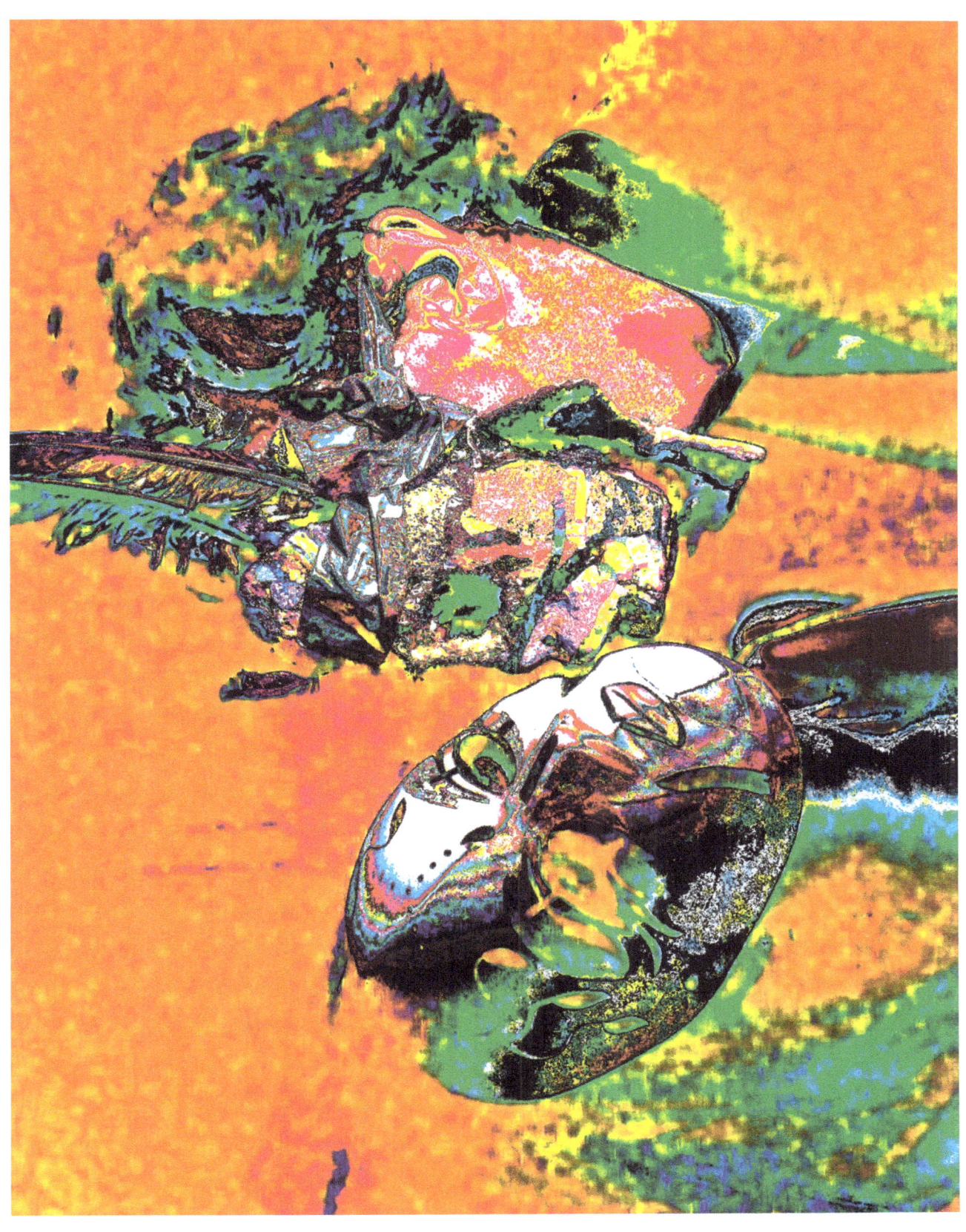

THE LOVERS (STOLEN LOVE) - (2015) photograph with Treatments

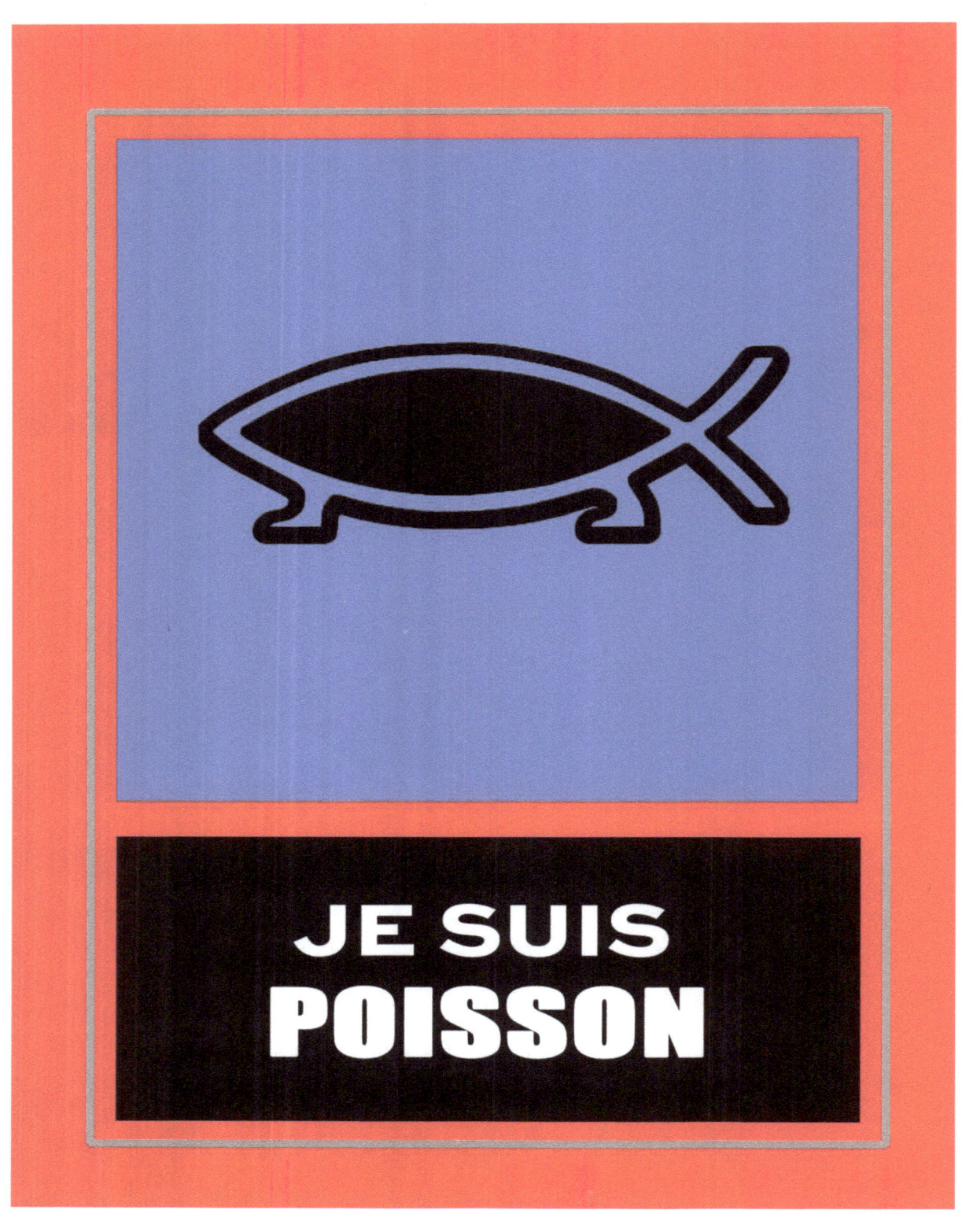

JE SUIS POISSON - (2014) graphic computer design

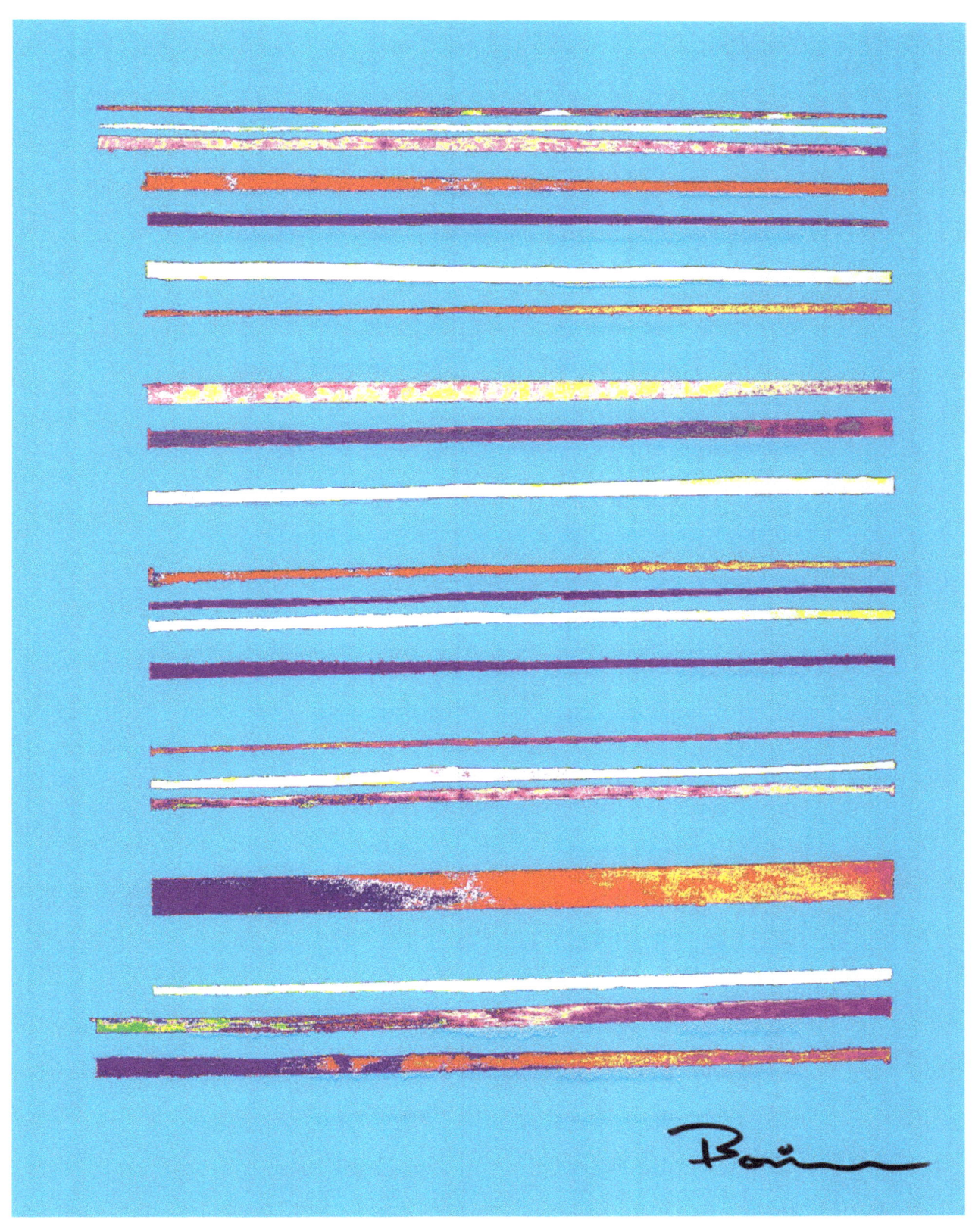

LINES IV (2001) acrylic and pencil on board mainly

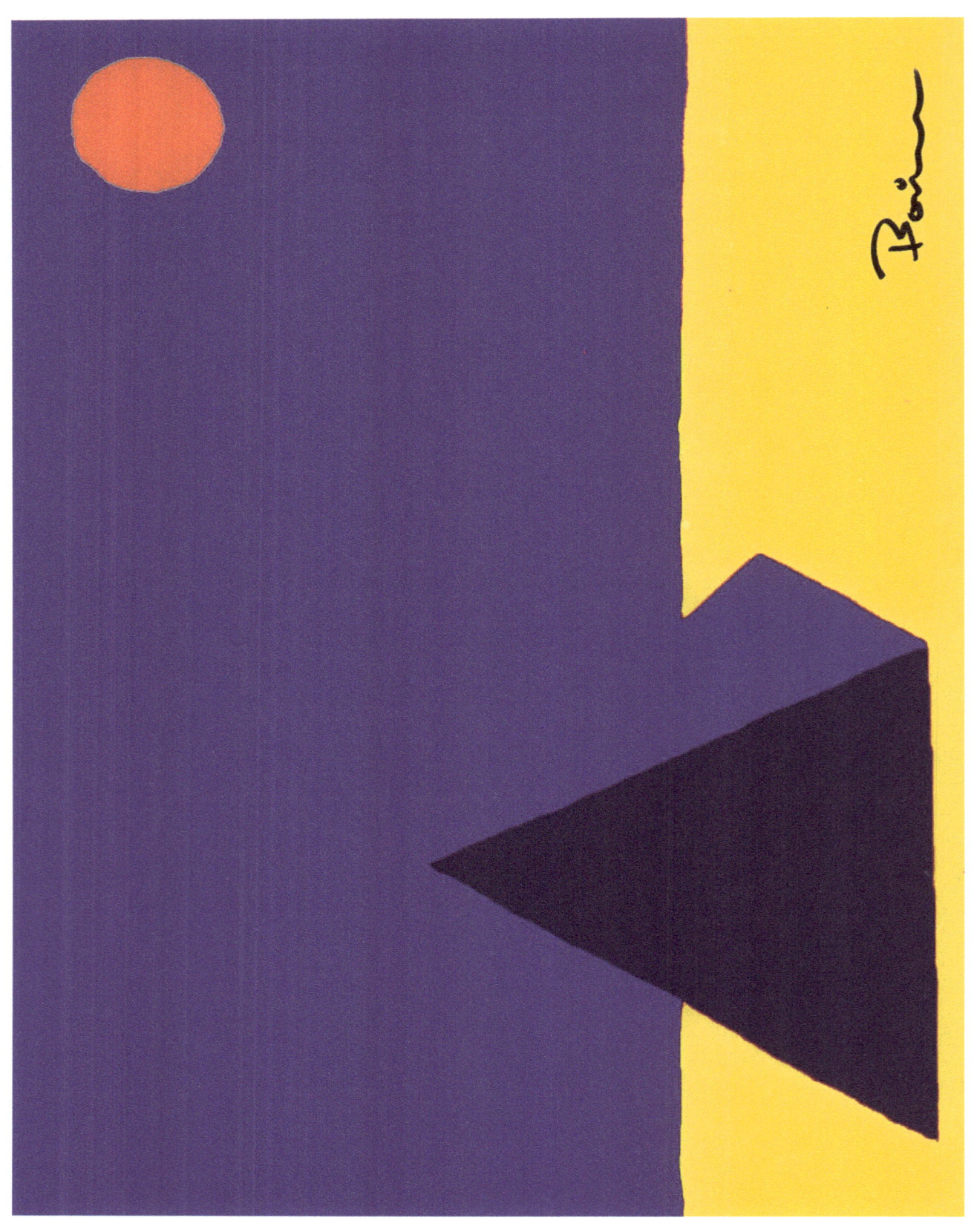

ONE'S INNER PYRAMID - (CIRCA 1988) acrylic on board

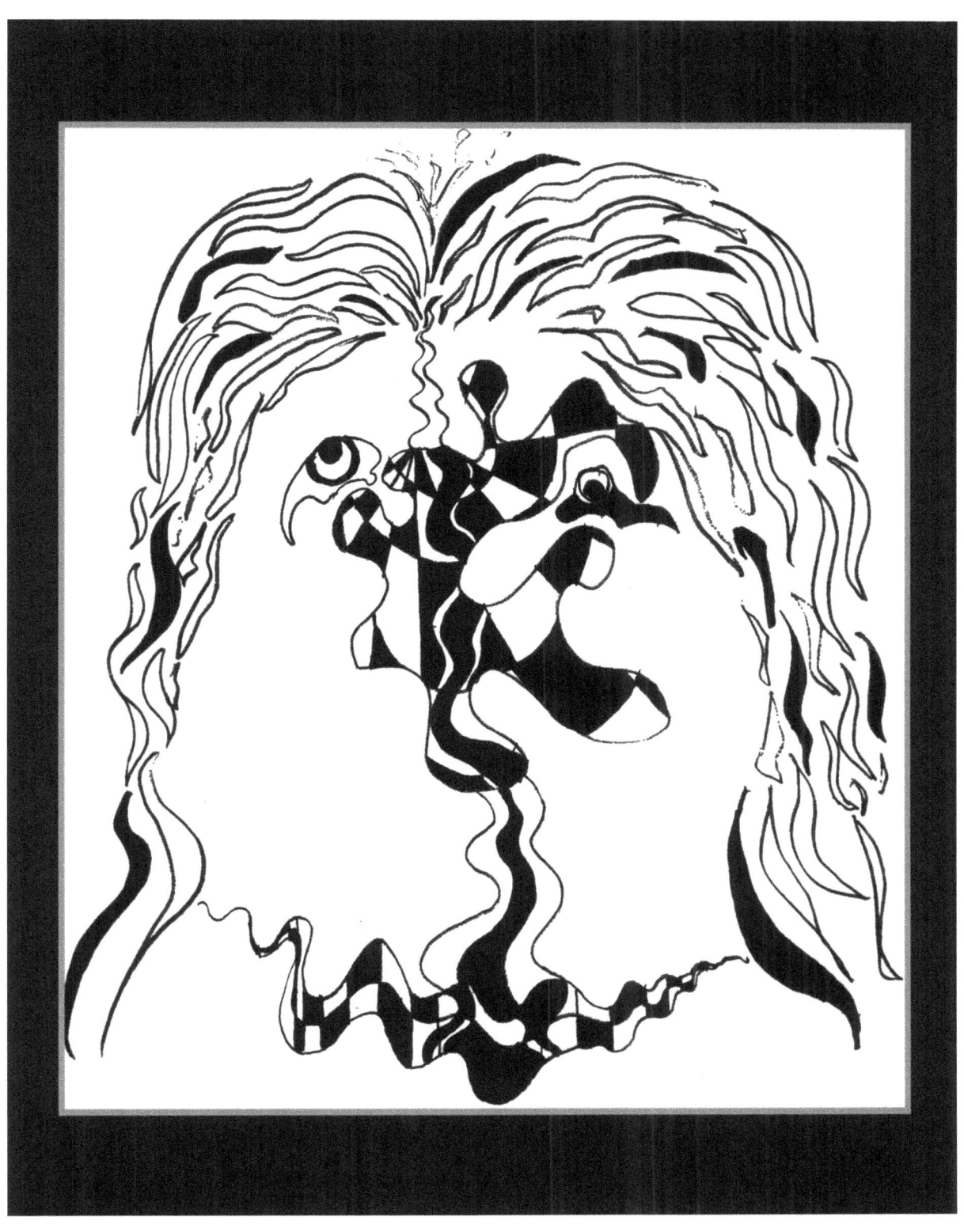

UNTITLED - (CIRCA 1984) mainly pencil

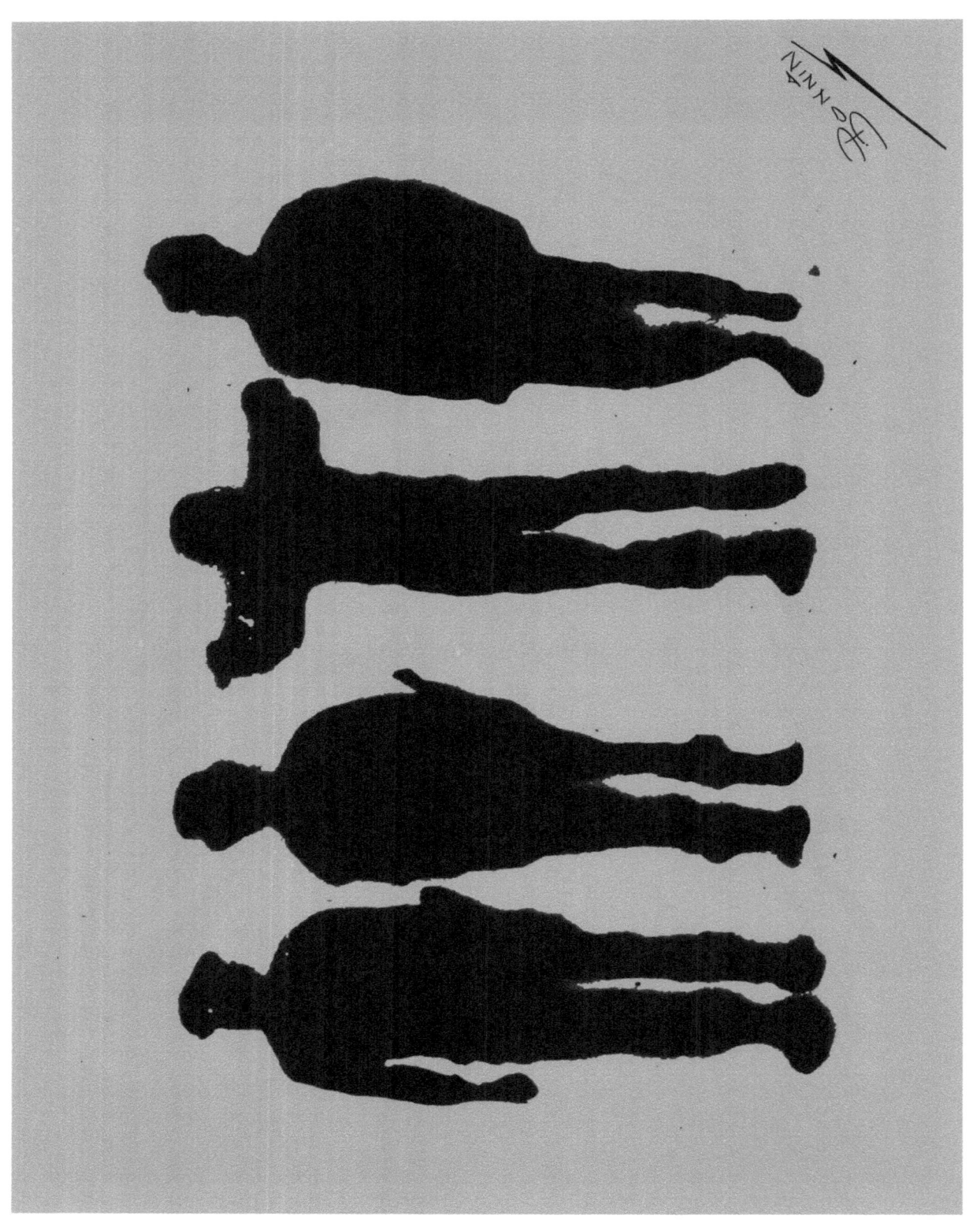

FOUR COMRADES - (UNDATED) technique unknown

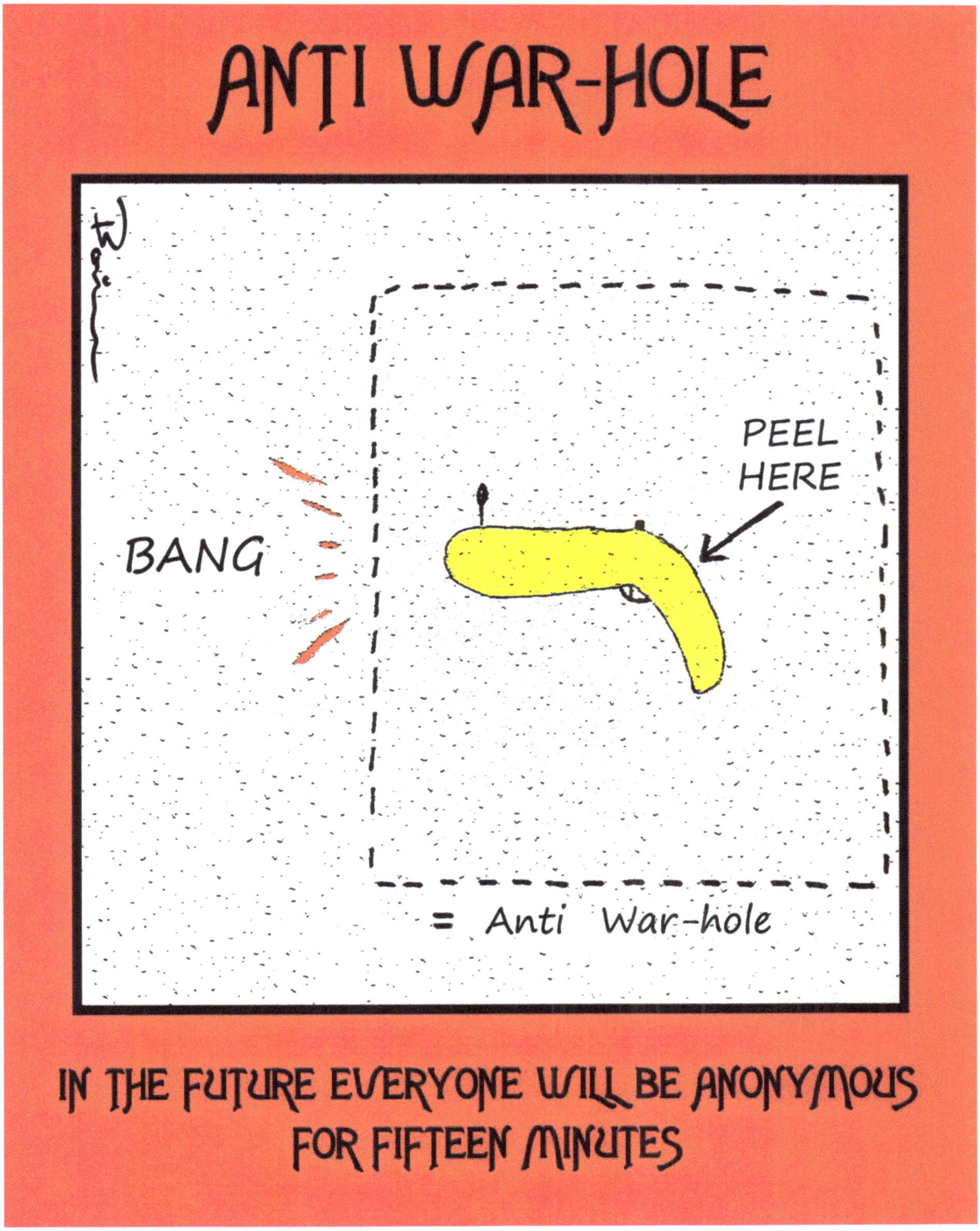

ANTI WAR-HOLE

BANG

PEEL HERE

= Anti War-hole

IN THE FUTURE EVERYONE WILL BE ANONYMOUS FOR FIFTEEN MINUTES

ANTI WAR-HOLE (CIRCA 2003) various techniques – beginning with acrylic on board

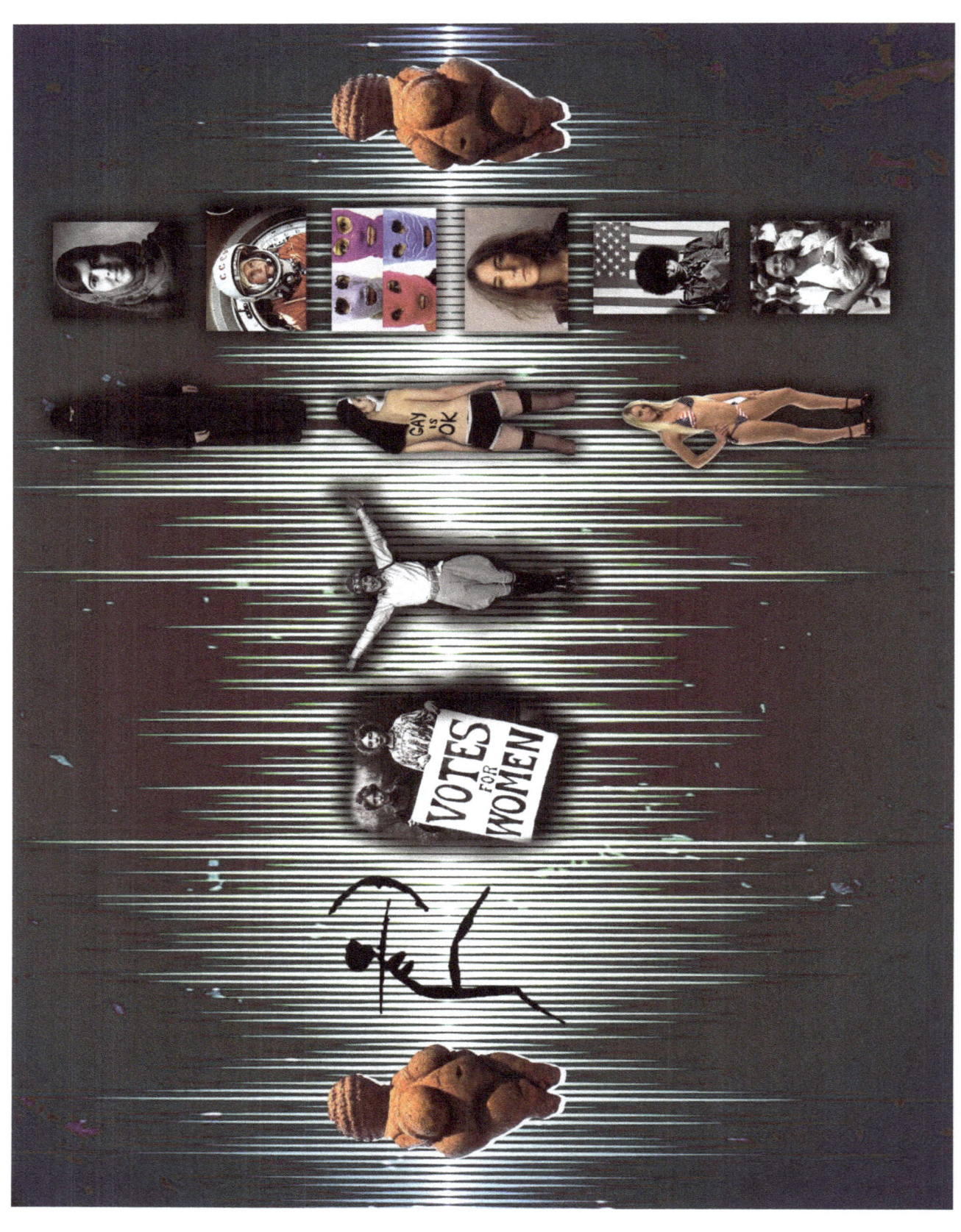

W-149-17X - (2018) various techniques

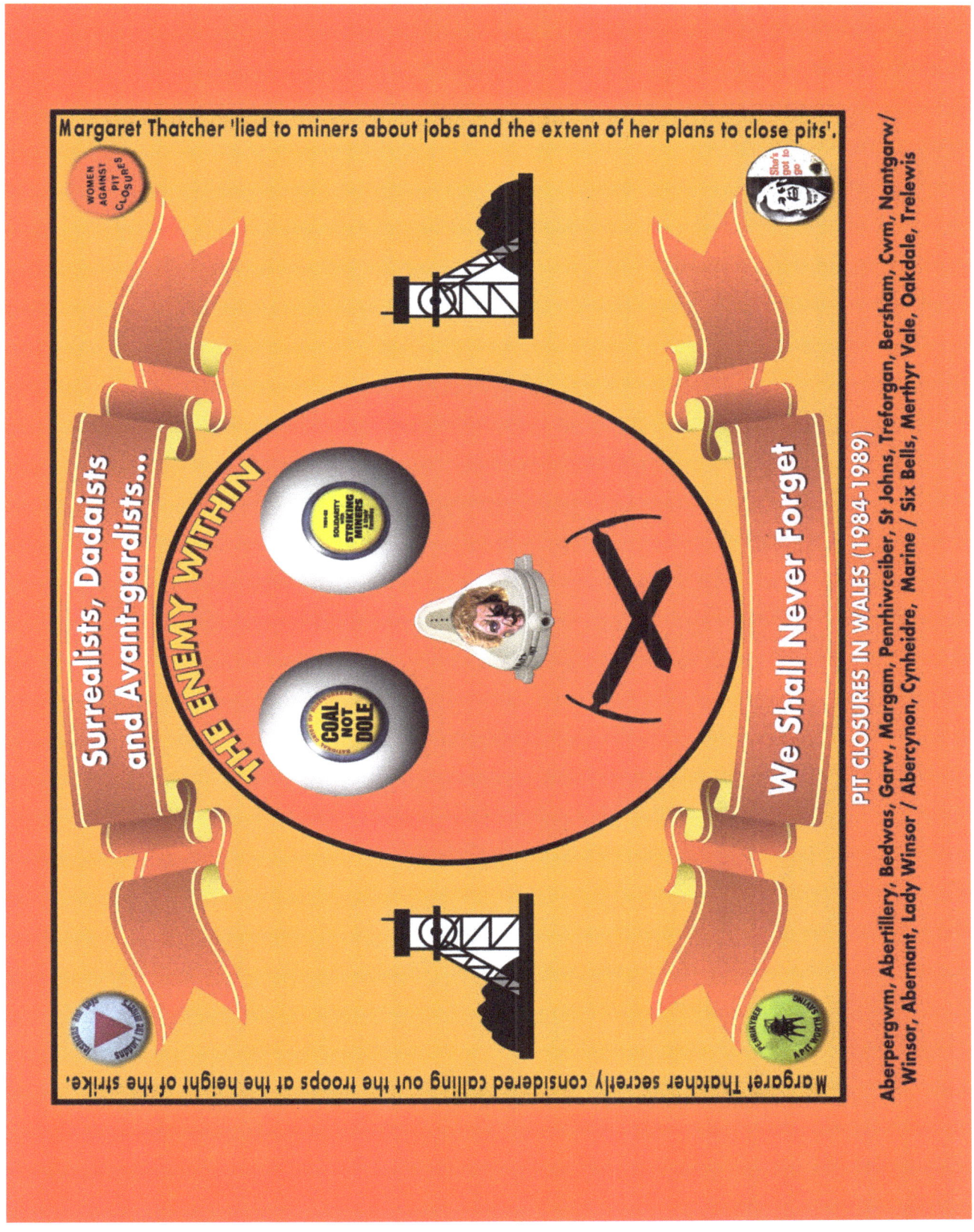

THE ENEMY WITHIN - (2018) various techniques

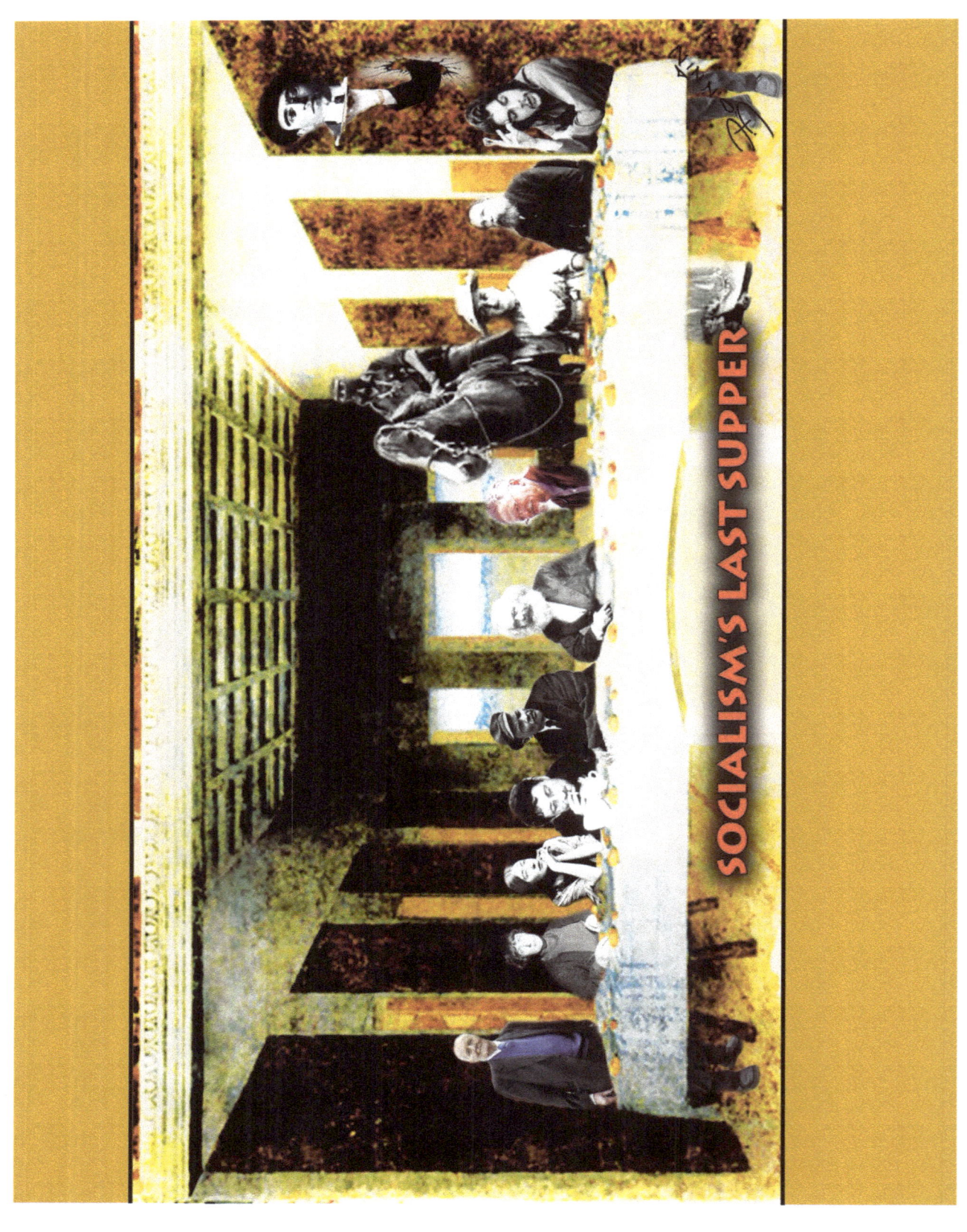

SOCIALISM'S LAST SUPPER - (2015) various techniques

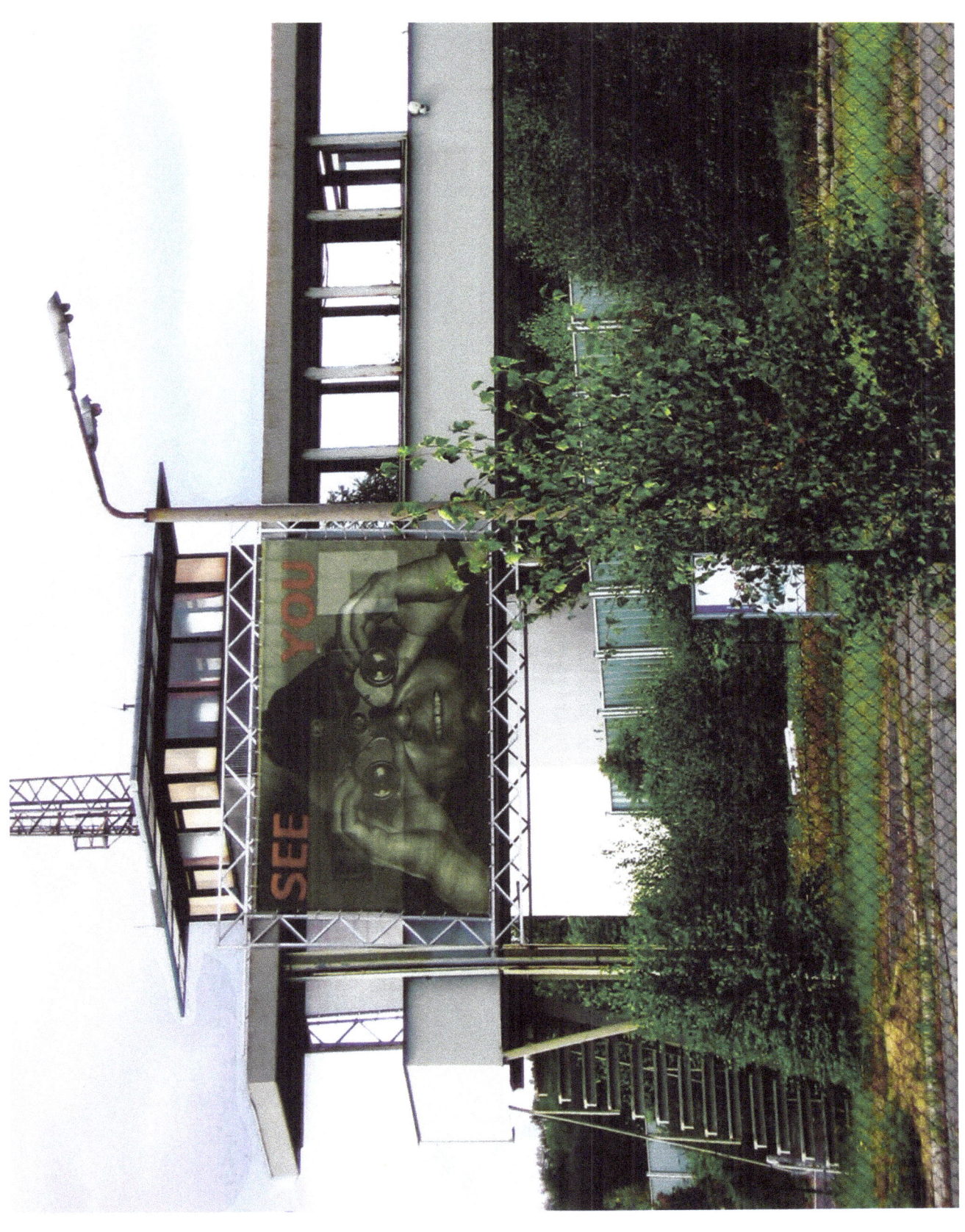

SEE YOU - (CIRCA **1988**) photograph

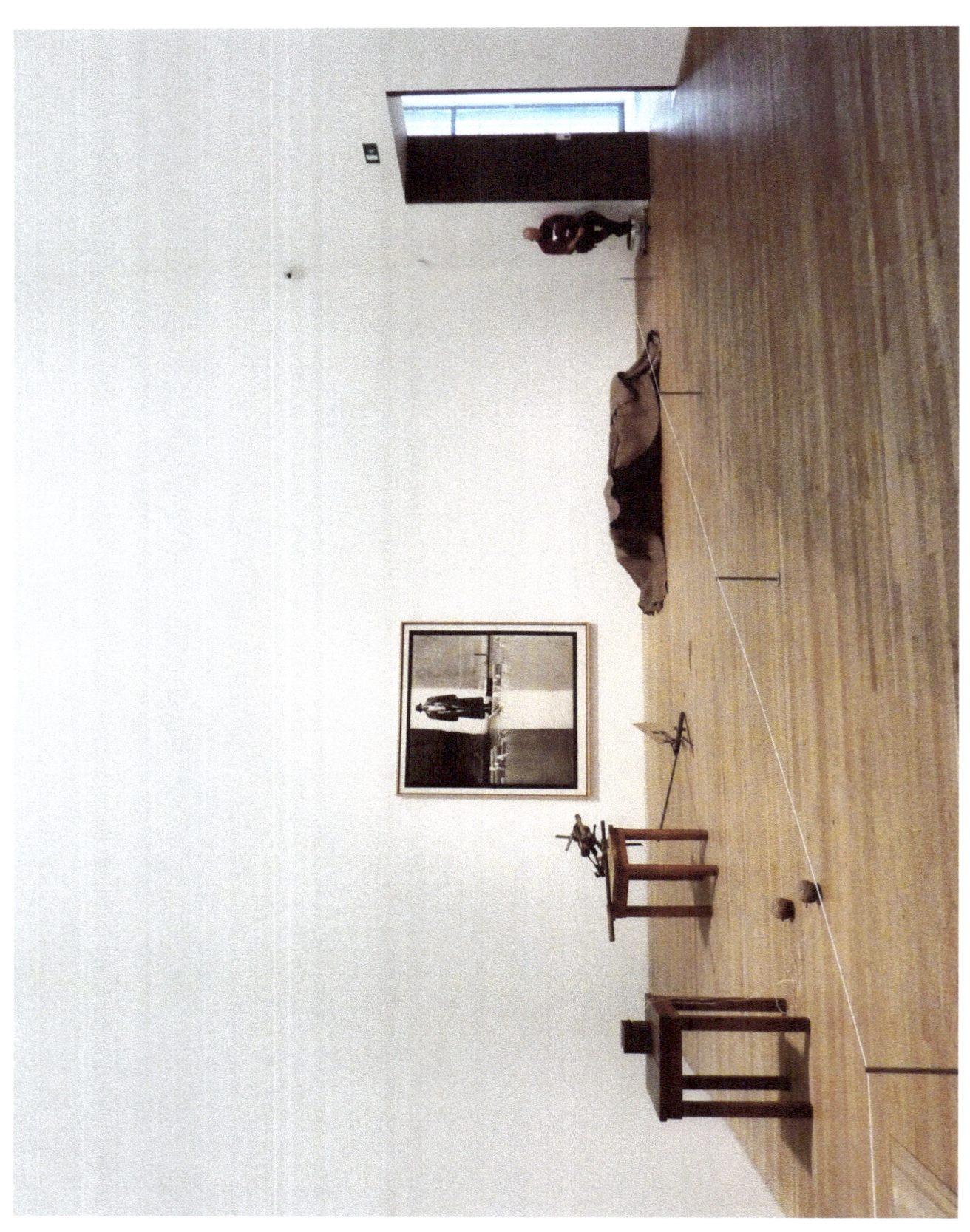

MAN AS ART - (2008) photograph

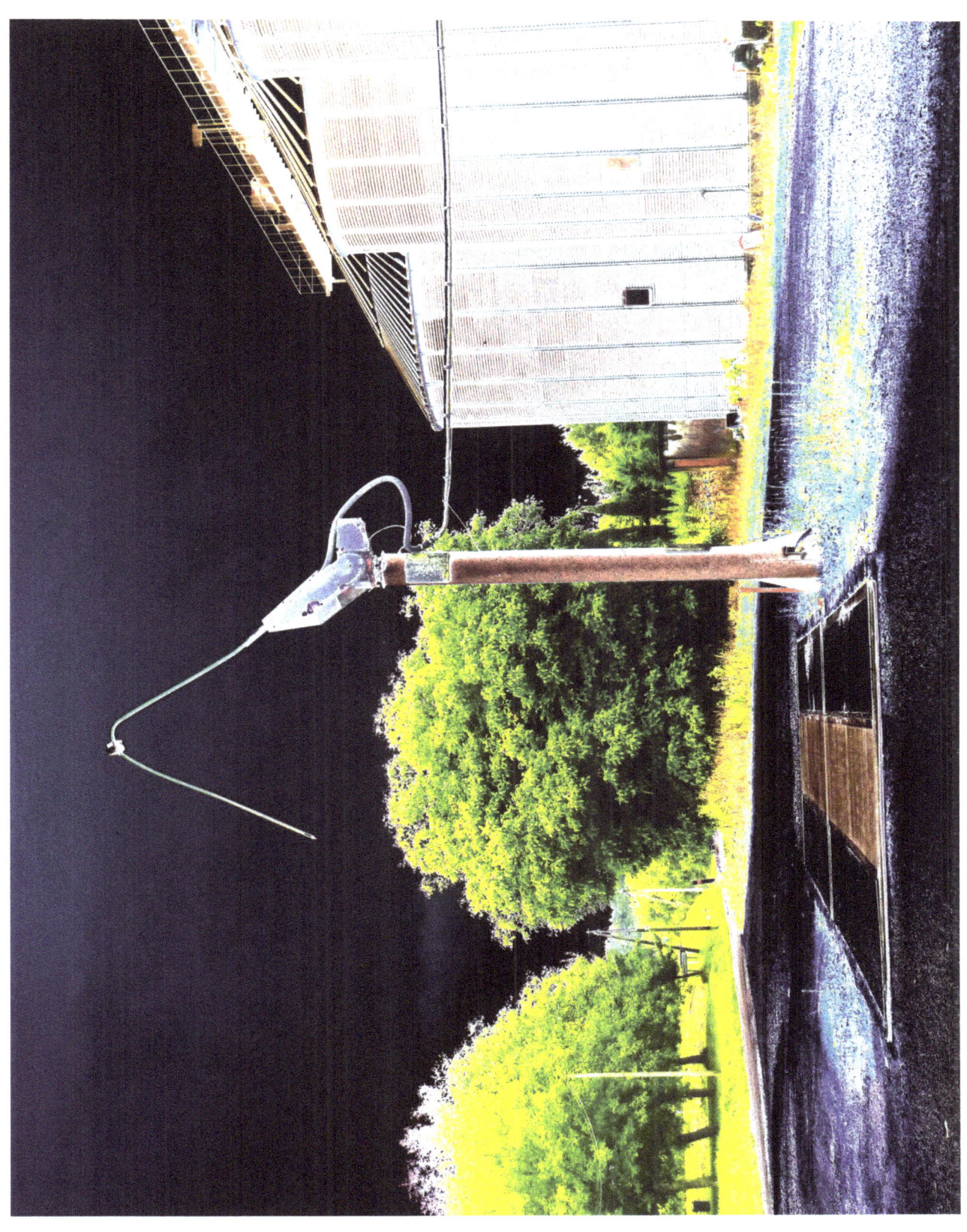

INDUSTRIAL BIRD IV - (2017) photograph with treatments

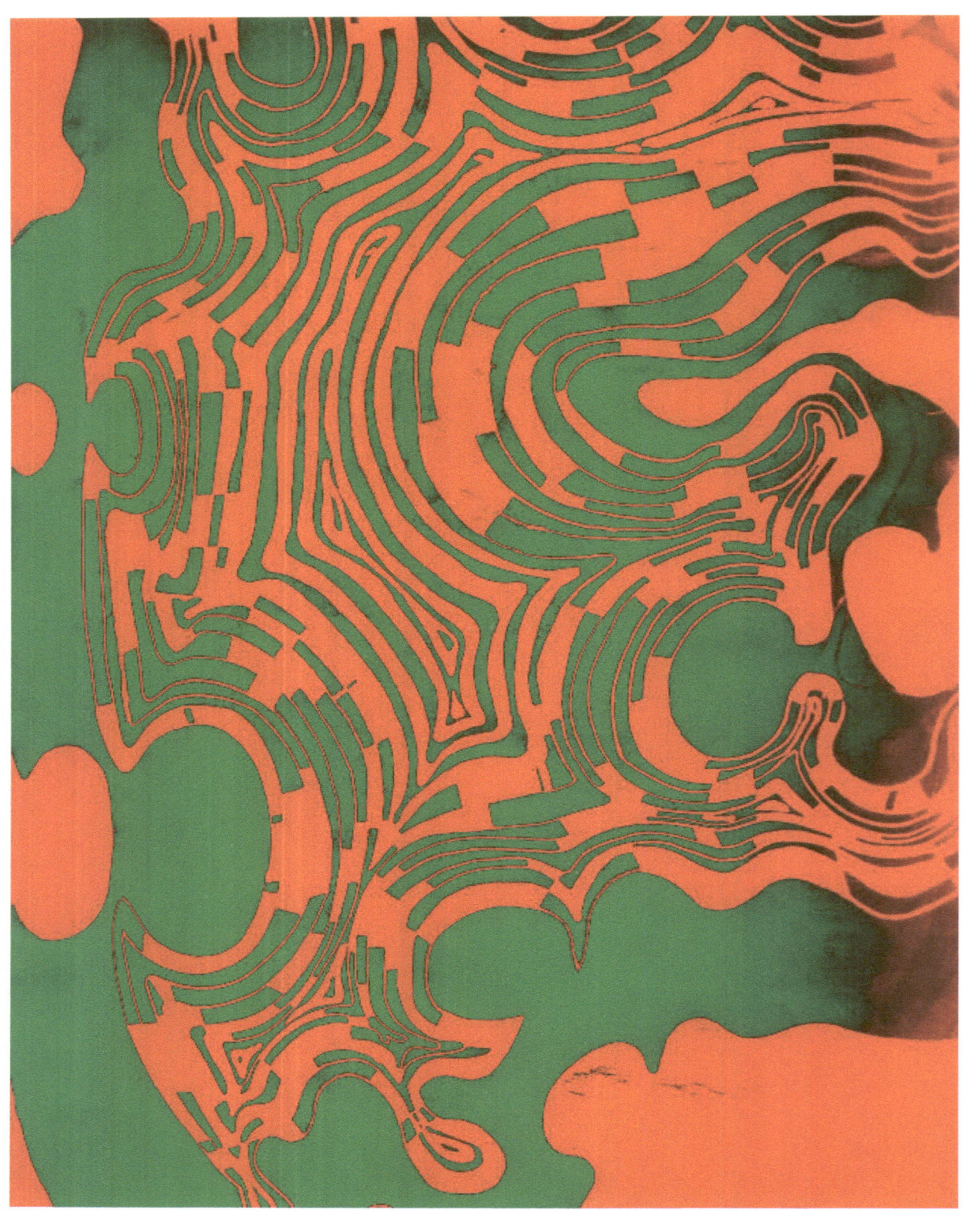

MIND MAZE - (1982 & 2004) pencil on paper initially, then photographed and treated

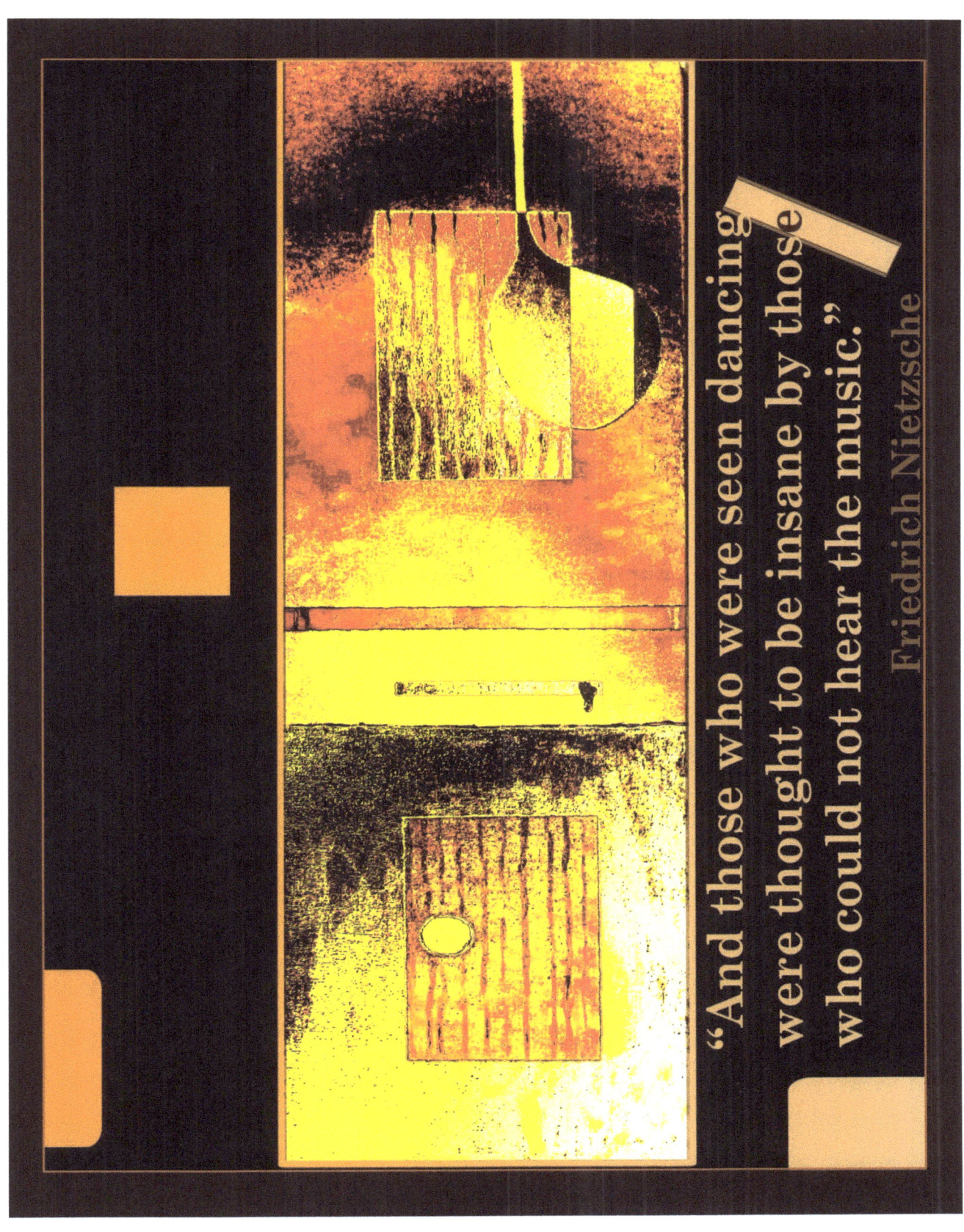

INVISIBLE TRUTH - (circa 1999 & circa 2004) initially a painting of acrylic on board, subsequently highly treated

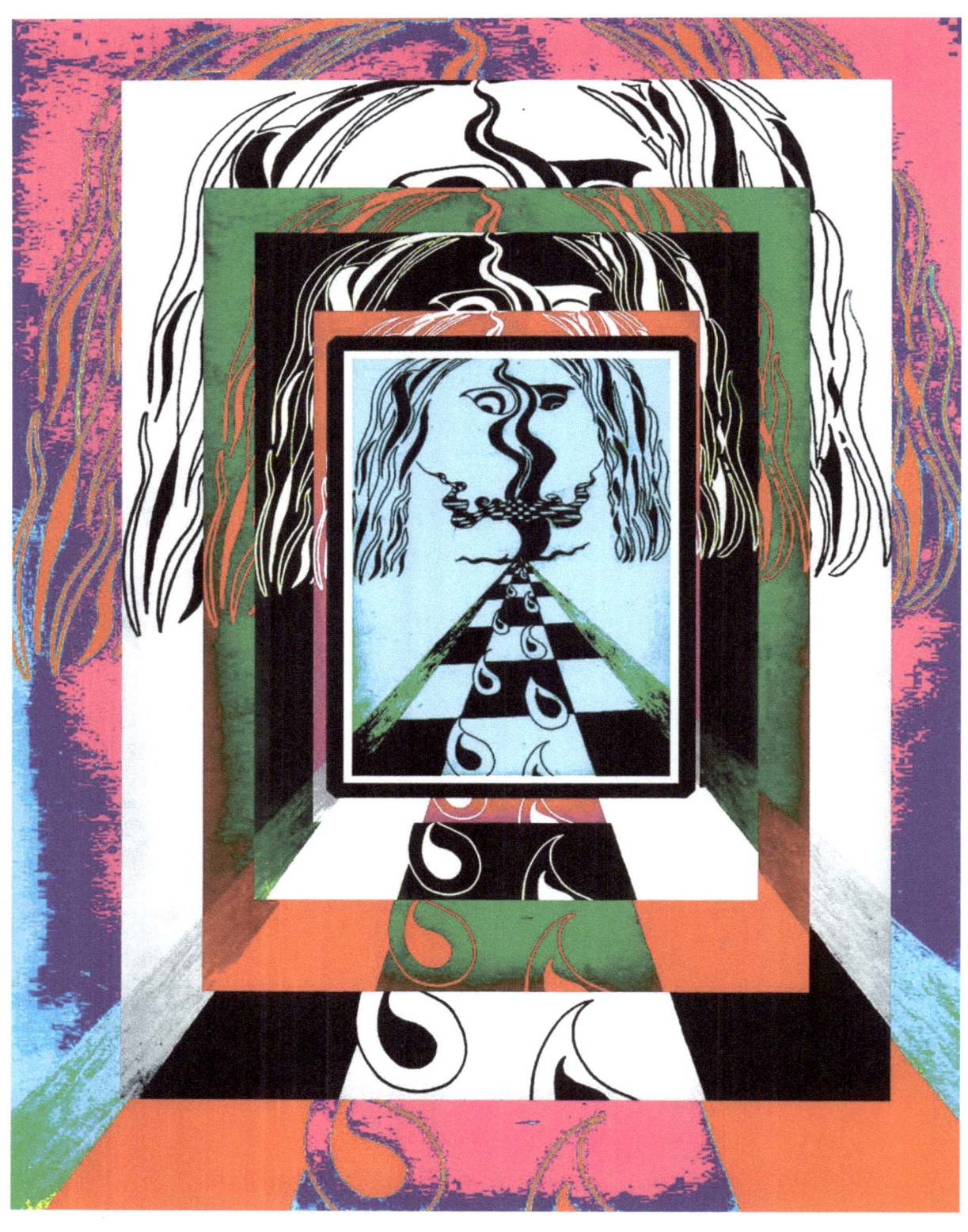

ONE-EYED FISH - (circa 1984 & circa 2004) initially a pencil drawing then subsequently with treatments

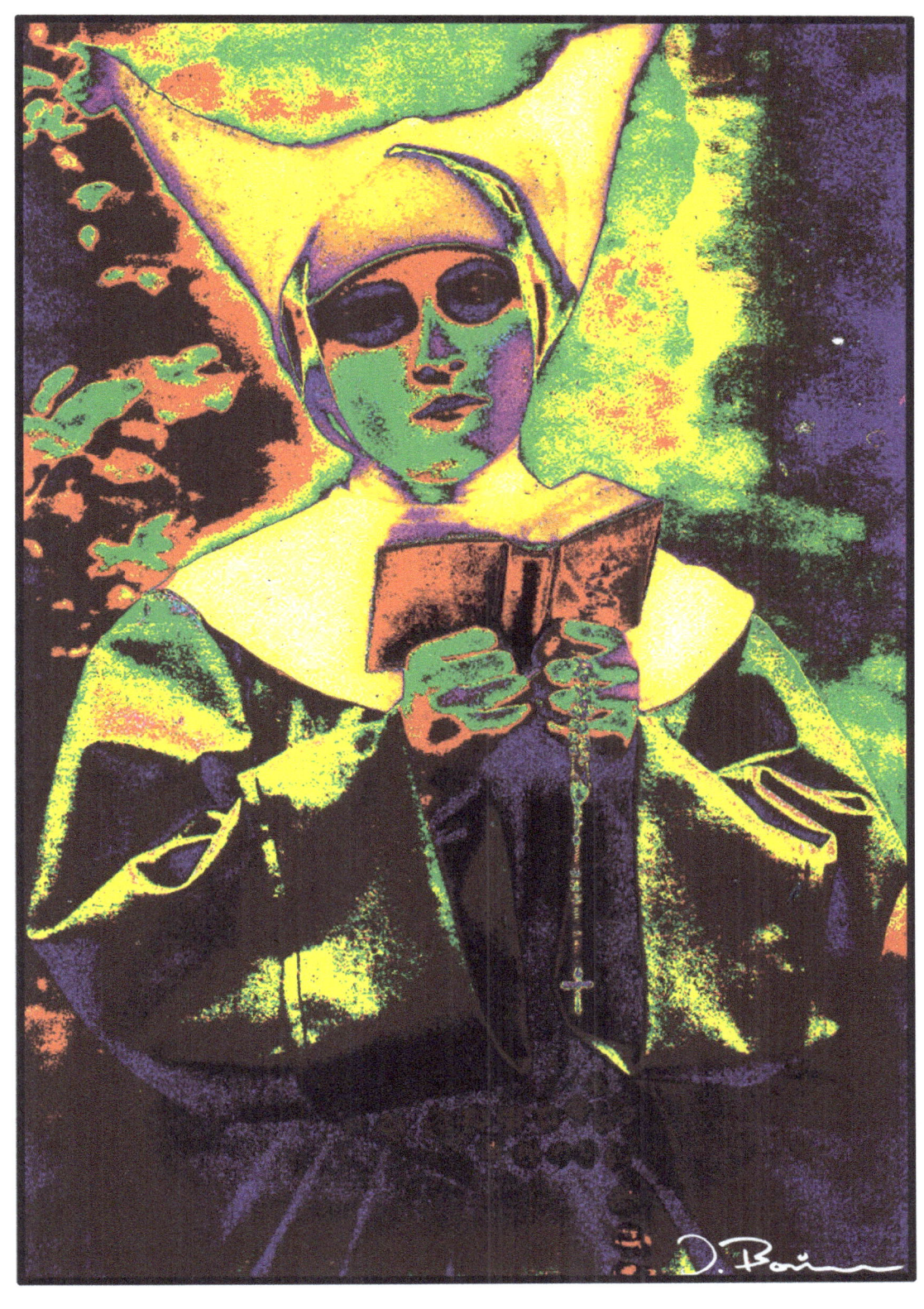

NUN THE WISER II - (2018) photograph and treatments

Books by Jean Bonnin

Novels:

A Certain Experience of the Impossible (2009)
Lines Within The Circle (2011)
The Cubist's House (2015)

Poetry/ Aphorisms:

Being and Somethingness (2015)
Beautiful Wilderness (2017)

Translations:

Magical Sense [by Malcolm de Chazal] (2015)
Magical Science [by Malcolm de Chazal] (2015)

Soon to be Published:

The Da-Dalí Code
One-Eyed Fish

For more information: www.redeggpublishing.com

THE SHOW IS OVER YOU MAY NOW GO HOME

www.ingramcontent.com/pod-product-compliance
Lightning Source LLC
Chambersburg PA
CBHW041546220526

45473CB00015B/2968